SONGS
OF INNOCENCE
AND OF
EXPERIENCE

TWENTIETH CENTURY INTERPRETATIONS
OF

SONGS
OF INNOCENCE
AND OF
EXPERIENCE

A Collection of Critical Essays

Edited by
MORTON D. PALEY

Prentice-Hall, Inc. *Englewood Cliffs, N. J.*

PRENTICE-HALL INTERNATIONAL, INC. (*London*)
PRENTICE-HALL OF AUSTRALIA, PTY. LTD. (*Sydney*)
PRENTICE-HALL OF CANADA, LTD. (*Toronto*)
PRENTICE-HALL OF INDIA PRIVATE LIMITED (*New Delhi*)
PRENTICE-HALL OF JAPAN, INC. (*Tokyo*)

For S. Foster Damon

A Note on References

Unless otherwise indicated, the page numbers for Blake's works used in the selections in this volume refer to *The Complete Writings of William Blake*, ed. Geoffrey Keynes (London and New York, 1957), or to the revised edition of that text published in the Oxford Standard Authors series (1966) and paginated identically.

Contents

Introduction

by Morton D. Paley

In 1789, William Blake published a book unique in several ways. Other poets, such as Isaac Watts and Anna Letitia Barbauld, had produced volumes of religious poems for children in the eighteenth century; and some books of this type, such as Christopher Smart's *Hymns for the Amusement of Children,* were emblem books with an illustration for each poem. Blake was alone, however, in producing *Songs of Innocence* as a total work of art comprising both design and text (including calligraphy). Even the process of relief etching by which the book was published was developed by Blake himself—with, according to a tradition established by Blake's contemporary John Thomas Smith, visionary assistance:

> Blake, after deeply perplexing himself as to the mode of accomplishing the publication of his illustrated songs, without their being subject to the expense of letter-press, his brother Robert stood before him in one of his visionary imaginations, and so decidedly directed him in the way in which he ought to proceed, that he immediately followed his advice, by writing his poetry, and drawing his marginal subjects of embellishments in outline upon the copper-plate with an impervious liquid, and then eating the plain parts or lights away with aquafortis considerably below them, so that the outlines were left as a stereotype. The plates in this state were then printed in any tint that he wished, to enable him or Mrs. Blake to colour the marginal figures up by hand in imitation of the drawings.[1]

As Alexander Gilchrist, author of the first book-length biography of Blake, said, "Never before so surely was a man literally the author of his own book." [2] A sequel, produced in the same way, was advertised in 1793, but no separate copy of *Songs of Experience* is known to exist.

[1] *Nollekens and His Times,* ed. Wilfred Whitten (London and New York, 1920), II, 372.

[2] *The Life of William Blake,* ed. Ruthven Todd, rev. ed. (London and New York, 1945), p. 61. (Gilchrist's *Life,* subtitled *Pictor Ignotus,* was first published in 1863.)

Instead, it was issued as part of a single volume with the earlier *Songs*, with a combined title page, etched in 1794: *Songs of Innocence and of Experience / Shewing the Two Contrary States of the Human Soul.* Clearly, Blake regarded the two sets of *Songs* as an artistic whole, and we shall increase our appreciation of the poems if we follow him in this.

What are the two Contrary States and what is the relationship between them? *Innocence* and *Experience* are not, first of all, a direct record of Blake's spiritual autobiography; for we would then have a poet who was Innocent at the age of thirty-two, when *Innocence* was published, but somehow became Experienced two years later when he began to write the second group of *Songs* in his Notebook. Anyone who thinks the *Songs of Innocence* reflect Blake's own world view at the time of composition should carefully read the prose satire *An Island in the Moon,* which Blake wrote in 1784 and in which versions of three *Songs of Innocence* first appear. In this anything-but-innocent narrative, the simplicity and pathos of "Holy Thursday," "Nurse's Song," and "The Little Boy Lost" contrast sharply with the egotism and pretentiousness of the characters. As if in recognition of this, after the first Song "they all sat silent for a quarter of an hour." [3] Of course we cannot know whether Blake had the *Songs of Experience* in mind when he wrote the *Songs of Innocence,* but we do know that four of the earlier group seemed to him sufficiently poems of Experience to be shifted to the latter group in 1794: "The School Boy," "The Little Girl Lost," "The Little Girl Found," and "The Voice of the Ancient Bard." These poems had already burst the bounds of the state of Innocence, all of them presenting themes more appropriate to the contrary State—institutional restraint, the prophetic function of the poet, the growth of self-awareness. Innocence *demands* Experience: both are phases in the spiritual development of man and, at the same time, perennial ways of looking at the world.

The state of Innocence is compounded of the pagan Age of Gold and the Judeo-Christian Eden. Externally and generically, it applies to the condition of man before the Fall; internally and psychologically to the child who has not yet experienced the inner divisions of human life. Its literary forebears are the worlds of the pastoral and the Psalms. Blake's Innocence also has a special relationship to the thought of the Swedish visionary Emanuel Swedenborg, whose works Blake annotated

---

[3] *The Poetry and Prose of William Blake,* ed. David V. Erdman (Garden City, N.Y., 1965), p. 453. This edition will hereafter be cited as E.

with great interest in the 1780's and who conceived of Innocence in terms peculiarly appropriate to Blake's:

> Afterwards genuine innocence was represented by a most beautiful child, naked and full of life; for the really innocent, who are in the inmost heaven and thus nearest to the Lord, always appear before the eyes of the other angels as children, and some of them naked; for innocence is represented by nakedness unaccompanied by shame, as is said of the first man and his wife in Paradise (*Gen.* ii, 25); so when their state of innocence perished they were ashamed of their nakedness and hid themselves. . . . In a word, the wiser the angels are, and the more innocent they are the more they appear to themselves as little children. This is why in the Word "childhood" signifies innocence. . . .[4]

Swedenborg's conception of Innocence as an inner state, taking images such as the child and the lamb as correspondences, has many correlatives in Blake. For example, Swedenborg says:

> In the Word also by *name* is signified the essence of a thing and by *seeing and calling by name* to know its quality.

> . . . It is evident that all innocence is from the Lord. For this reason the Lord is called in the Word a "lamb," a lamb signifying innocence.

> The Lord himself is called *a child*, or a *little boy* (Isaiah ix.6), because he is innocence itself and love itself.[5]

Blake condensed the meanings of such passages as these in "The Lamb" (E, p. 8):

> He is called by thy name,
> For he calls himself a Lamb:
> He is meek & he is mild,
> He became a little child:
> I a child & thou a lamb,
> We are called by his name.

Many other Swedenborgian echoes could be traced in the *Songs of Innocence,* especially in such hymn-like poems as "A Cradle Song" and "The Divine Image," but what concerns us here is not so much specific sources as the fact that for both Blake and Swedenborg the

---

[4] *Heaven and Its Wonders and Hell* (New York, 1956), pp. 218–19. This book, first published in English translation in 1784, was owned and annotated by Blake.

[5] *Arcana Cœlestia* (New York, 1873), I, 54; *Heaven and Hell,* p. 174; *Arcana,* I, 146. Volume I of the *Arcana* was first published in English in 1784.

state of Innocence is projected in terms of images corresponding to an inner, spiritual condition:

> This World is also full of Correspondences, and so likewise is the Hellish Kingdom. To give only a Hint by Way of Illustration. To two Angels conversing together, supposing on Love or Innocence, the corresponding visible Scene presented to them may be delightful Fields with sporting Lambs, little Children playing in Flower-Gardens, warbling Birds of beautiful Colours, and the like pleasing Imagery. To Infernal Spirits, according to their different States and Employments respectively, are represented Scenes of Wildness, Barrenness, Dismay, or Horror.[6]

Experience, too, is an inner state externalized in a world of images—chain, thorns, spears, graves, briars, blood, and roots, to name a few—all of which correspond to felt qualities in life. As Blake says in the "Motto to the Songs of Innocence & of Experience," which he wrote in his Notebook but did not publish, "Experience teaches them ['The Good'] to catch / And to cage the Fairies & Elves" (E, p. 490). The Fairies and Elves represent spontaneous, instinctual joy and knowledge (cf. the fairies in "William Bond," which depart from William and are replaced by Angels of Providence). In Experience, which is the world of normal adult life, people try to analyze and codify their feelings, and as a result they become incapable of spontaneity. Like the speaker of "The Angel," they suppress their real selves out of fear; like the Sunflower, they defer gratification to a "sweet golden clime" which is actually "an allegorical abode where existence hath never come" (*Europe* [1794]; E, p. 61). The traditional hierarchy of society, seen as benevolent in *Innocence*, is now regarded as a vast exploitative deceit: "God & his Priest & King / Who make up a heaven of our misery" (E, p. 23). The pastoral landscape of Innocence is replaced by the *paysage moralisé* of wartime London, a city of victims. With all this suffering, however, Experience also brings a bitter wisdom:

> What is the price of Experience do men buy it for a song
> Or wisdom for a dance in the street? No it is bought with the price
> Of all that a man hath his house his wife his children
> Wisdom is sold in the desolate market where none come to buy
> And in the witherd field where the farmer plows for bread in vain

> (*Four Zoas*, 35:11–15; E, p. 318)

Experience, then, is not wholly negative. The harmony of Innocence

[6] Emanuel Swedenborg, *A Treatise of the Nature of Influx*, 3d ed. (London, 1788), p. 59*n*.

has been lost, but insight comes in its place. In the wisdom of Experience, as embodied in the voice of the prophetic Bard at the beginning and again at the end of the second group of *Songs*, lies the possibility of reorganizing man's divided self and, if not of regaining the lost world of Innocence, then of forging a new unity. "Man is so created," Swedenborg wrote, "as to be during his childhood in external innocence, and when he becomes old in internal innocence, to the end that he may come by means of the former into the latter, and from the latter return into the former" (*Heaven and Hell*, p. 171). "Unorganiz'd Innocence," according to Blake, is "An Impossibility. Innocence dwells with Wisdom, but never with Ignorance." [7]

The transition from Innocence to Experience may be seen as a version of what medieval theologians called the Fortunate Fall—the idea that the fall of Adam and Eve was in a paradoxical sense a "happy sin," in that otherwise Christ would not have been born to save mankind. For Blake, the fall into Experience was if not happy at least necessary, as may be seen in the three longer poems he wrote from 1789 to 1793: *Tiriel*, *The Book of Thel*, and *Visions of the Daughters of Albion*. All three are in some part concerned with the relation between Innocence and Experience. *Tiriel* (written ca. 1789 and never published) takes place in a world ruled by a tyrannical father, whose closing lament expresses the sense of anguish that informs *Experience*; some lines are particularly close to "Infant Sorrow" (and also to the longer Notebook poem from which it derives):

> The Child springs from the womb, the father ready stands to form
> The infant head while the mother idle plays with her dog on her couch
> The young bosom is cold for lack of mothers nourishment & milk
> Is cut off from the weeping mouth with difficulty & pain
> The little lids are lifted & the little nostrils opend
> The father forms a whip to rouze the sluggish senses to act
> And scourges off all youthful fancies from the new-born man
> Then walks the weak infant in sorrow compelld to number footsteps
> Upon the sand.
>
> (*Tiriel*, 8:12–20; E, pp. 281–82)

Infant Sorrow
My mother groand! my father wept.
Into the dangerous world I leapt:

[7] *The Complete Writings of William Blake*, ed. Sir Geoffrey Keynes (London, 1966), p. 380.

Helpless, naked, piping loud;
Like a fiend hid in a cloud.

Struggling in my fathers hands:
Striving against my swadling bands:
Bound and weary I thought best
To sulk upon my mothers breast.

(E, p. 28)

In Tiriel's world, Innocence exists only as a debased caricature, in form
of two senile figures, Har and Heva. This childish couple, who seem
to represent the arts as Blake regarded them in his day, spend their
time in a parody of Innocent pursuits:

For we have many sports to shew thee & many songs to sing
And after dinner we will walk into the cage of Har
And thou shal help us to catch birds. & gather them ripe cherries

(3:11–13; E, p. 276)

Having evaded the painful awareness of Experience, they have failed
to achieve mature identity, and so are impotent and irrelevant:

But they were as the shadow of Har. & as the years forgotten
Playing with flowers. & running after birds they spent the day
And in the night like infants slept delighted with infant dreams

(2:7–9; E, p. 274)

A similar fate is risked by the heroine of *The Book of Thel* (which
bears 1789 on its title page but which may not have been completed
until 1791; see E, p. 713). Thel, whose name is the Greek root for
"will," lives in the pastoral world that Blake will later call Beulah.
Her time has come to enter the world below, the world of Generation or Experience. Already wracked by the consciousness of mortality
that this new state brings, she wants desperately to protract her
sheltered happiness. Four embodiments of universal life—the Lilly,
the Cloud, the Worm, and the Clod of Clay—assure her that "we live
not for ourselves," that the fragmentation of Experience is illusory.
Nevertheless, she is horrified by the limitations on physical and emotional existence in the lower world:

Why cannot the Ear be closed to its own destruction?
Or the glistning Eye to the poison of a smile!
Why are Eyelids stord with arrows ready drawn,
Where a thousand fighting men in ambush lie?

Or an Eye of gifts & graces, show'ring fruits & coined gold!
Why a Tongue impress'd with honey from every wind?
Why an Ear, a whirlpool fierce to draw creations in?
Why a Nostril wide inhaling terror trembling & affright
Why a tender curb upon the youthful burning boy!
Why a little curtain of flesh on the bed of our desire?

(*Thel*, 6:11–20; E, p. 6)

These lines remind us of the same theme as expressed in such *Songs of Experience* as "The Angel" and "To Tirzah":

I dried my tears & armd my fears,
With ten thousand shields and spears.

(11–12; E, p. 24)

Thou Mother of my Mortal part
With cruelty didst mould my Heart,
And with false self-decieving tears,
Didst bind my Nostrils Eyes & Ears.

Didst close my Tongue in senseless clay
And me to Mortal Life betray:

(8–14; E, p. 30)

In contrast to Thel, who "with a shriek. / Fled back unhinderd till she came into the vales of Har" (6:21–22; E, p. 6), the heroine of *Visions of the Daughters of Albion* (1793) has the courage to confront Experience. Oothoon, though raped by the puritanical hypocrite Bromion and rejected by her self-preoccupied lover Theotormon, can yet declare the sanctity of bodily love. She embodies the triumph of Innocence *in* Experience, just as in the dark world of *Lear,* Cordelia redeems Nature from the general curse. In a triumphant assertion, she brings together imagery from the two contrary worlds:

Sweetest the fruit that the worm feeds on. & the soul prey'd on by woe
The new wash'd lamb ting'd with the village smoke & the bright swan
By the red earth of our immortal river: . . .

(3:17–19; E, p. 46)

In his *Life Against Death: The Psychoanalytical Meaning of History* (Middletown, Conn., 1959), Norman O. Brown remarks:

It is one of the great romantic visions, clearly formulated by Schiller and Herder as early as 1793 and still vital in the systems of Hegel and Marx, that the history of mankind consists in a departure from a condition of undifferentiated primal unity with himself and with nature, an intermediate period in which man's powers are developed through differentiation and antagonism (alienation) with himself and with nature, and a final return to a unity on a higher level or harmony. . . .   (p. 86)

Blake's *Songs* is one of the first literary works to deliberately embody this pattern. Innocence and Experience are Contraries, and, as Blake tells us in *The Marriage of Heaven and Hell* (1790–93?), "without Contraries is no progression." In this case, progression is toward a condition of being in which the harmony lost in the fall from Innocence is regained. The agent of regeneration is Energy, characterized in *The Marriage* as "the only life" (E, p. 34). In the fallen world of Experience, this Energy is present as the wrath of the Tyger, for, as David V. Erdman says, "The very process of the creation of the tiger brings about the condition of freedom in which his enemies (his prey) become his friends, as angels become devils in *The Marriage*." [8] According to the myth Blake created in his longer poems of 1793–95, the Energy liberated in the American and the French Revolutions is to transform the conditions of human life.

> Fires inwrap the earthly globe, yet man is not consumd;
> Amidst the lustful fires he walks: his feet become like brass,
> His knees and thighs like silver, & his breast and head like gold.
>
> *(America, 8:15–17; E, p. 53)*

Orc, the Promethean "human fire" who defeats the armies of tyranny, declares an end to the institutional repression which characterizes the world of Experience—to slavery, exploitation, imprisonment, sexual bondage—"For Empire is no more, and now the Lion & Wolf shall cease" (6:15; E, p. 52). As we can see from *The Marriage* and *America,* works contemporary with the composition and publication of *Songs of Experience,* the world view of Experience, like that of Innocence, is not to be conceived as an end in itself. It is part of a dialectic that finds its synthesis in the regeneration of man. In Blake's later epics—*The Four Zoas, Milton,* and *Jerusalem*—the agent of regeneration becomes the visionary Imagination, as Blake, disillusioned with the failure of the French Revolution, turns inward for a solution. However, the dialectical structure remains: each of these long poems involves the loss of a Paradise "where we delight in innocence before the face of the Lamb"

---

[8] *Blake: Prophet Against Empire* (Princeton, 1954), p. 179.

(*Jerusalem*; E, p. 163), a period of "incessant pangs ages on ages / In Enmity & war" (*Four Zoas*; E, p. 380) and a regenerate state in which "all things are changd even as in ancient times" (*Four Zoas*; E, p. 391). The *Songs* are implicitly dialectical, the prophetic works explicitly so.

Although Blake's long poems are at last receiving the critical attention they deserve, it is probably through the *Songs* that Blake will continue to be known to most readers. In thinking about these poems, we should be aware of our own literary assumptions and the limitations that ensue, just as we are aware of our predecessors'. The Victorians at times mistook Blake's simplicity for naïveté and were, accordingly, disposed toward an overly literal view of the poems. We, by contrast, may be tempted to find complexities that are not there, to over-read, to discover myths hidden in the shrubbery as if the poem were an ingenious puzzle. The irony of the *Songs* is straightforward (the use of "charter'd" in "London," for example). Symbolism, when it occurs in one of these poems, is usually evident in its main structure (the worm in the sick rose), not hidden away in a sub-basement. Especially in considering lyric poetry, we should avoid equating the profound with the complicated. Blake's book is, indeed, rich in meaning and full of reverberation; as readers, we must distinguish between intelligent response and pedantic elaboration. The essays in this anthology will show what some interpreters of Blake have found in the *Songs*. It is hoped that they will stimulate the reader to make and to criticize his own interpretations, to take up the end of Blake's golden string himself, as Blake would have him do.

PART ONE

Interpretations

Metrics: Pattern and Variation

by Alicia Ostriker

How Wide the Gulf & Unpassable!
between Simplicity & Insipidity.
(Mirror-writing, M[*ilton*] p. 518)

There is a Buddhist proverb which explains the three stages of wisdom as follows. When you are unenlightened, mountains are mountains and rivers are rivers. As you approach Enlightenment, mountains are not mountains and rivers are not rivers. When you have achieved Enlightenment, mountains are mountains and rivers are rivers.

One's reactions to Blake's *Songs* follow a similar curve. First there is the surface delight. Then we discover that every symbol in these poems has a precise philosophical meaning, and we try to explain the songs in terms of Blake's system. We call this "understanding." Finally, there is again the surface. It is the same with Blake's versification. The immediate impression his verse makes on an unprepared reader will resemble that of jingle. It will seem extremely simple and obvious, providing the same sensuous pleasure which children's rhymes provide. Then the reader will discover that the poetry contains a good deal of formal variation and irregularity, and that the variations not only keep the verse from cloying, but contribute as far as rhythm and sound can do to the establishment of precise meanings. We must analyze their deviations from rhythmic norm. Yet this sort of analysis does not complete our understanding, since we must always return at last to the physical and emotional appeal of Blake's simplicity. Swinburne believed that "the . . . faculty of being right, proper to great lyrical

"*Metrics: Pattern and Variation*" *by Alicia Ostriker. From* Vision and Verse in William Blake (*Madison: University of Wisconsin Press, 1965*), *pp. 55–78. Reprinted by permission of the publisher.*

poets, was always an especial quality of Blake's. To go the right way and do the right thing, was in the nature of his metrical gift." [1] He did not elaborate on this feeling. But we can see that Blake's lyric rightness depends on a continual interplay between a primitive regularity which identifies Blake's world with the child's, and a functional irregularity which is the man's work.

The surface naïveté in Blake's metrics associates naturally with the same quality in his language. In diction, simplicity asserts itself through his plain Anglo-Saxon vocabulary, his uncomplicated sentence-structure, and his very heavy use of repetition. Metrically, it is revealed in the two areas of stanza-form and rhythmic beat.

First we can consider the naïveté of language. The most conspicuous stylistic feature of the *Songs* is their extraordinary use of repetition and parallel phrasing. Josephine Miles has found that in a thousand lines taken from Blake's whole poetic work some seventy or eighty nouns, adjectives, and verbs will appear more than ten times, instead of the thirty or forty common to other poets.[2] Actually, the concentration is greater than this implies, for Blake repeats some words in the *Songs* which scarcely reappear in the Prophetic Books, and, conversely, many ubiquitous prophetic favorites like "terrific" make no appearance in the *Songs.*

In *Innocence,* the following words (or variants of them) all occur over ten times: bird, child, infant, lamb, little, laugh, mother, father, sweet. Weep, sleep, and joy occur over twenty times. Blake portrays the infant's and child's world by suggesting the child's limited, intense, and affective vocabulary. Some of these words are distributed evenly through the lyrics, but intensity is also heightened by clustering in single poems, by the "Piping down . . . Piping songs . . . Pipe a song . . . Piper pipe" of the "Introduction," the "Merry Merry Sparrow . . . Pretty Pretty Robin" of "The Blossom," the bare "weep weep weep weep" of "The Chimney Sweeper," the "green woods laugh . . . air does laugh . . . green hill laughs . . . meadows laugh" of "Laughing Song," the "Sweet dreams . . . Sweet sleep . . . Sweet smiles . . . Sweet moans . . . Sleep sleep" of "A Cradle Song." You cannot look anywhere in *Songs of Innocence* without finding these hypnotic repetitions. Then, reinforcing them, you find parallel structures of phrase. "So I piped . . . So I sung . . . And I made . . . And I stain'd . . .

---

[1] Algernon Charles Swinburne, *William Blake, a Critical Essay* (London, 1906), p. 148.

[2] Josephine Miles, *Eras and Modes in English Poetry* (Berkeley, 1957), p. 79.

And I wrote" defines the process of creation in the "Introduction,"
and things are typically this simple for Blake. "By the stream & o'er
the mead," "I a child & thou a lamb," "Comfort in morning joy in the
noonday," "My mother died . . . and my father sold me," "I love to
rise in a summer morn . . . But to go to school in a summer morn,"
"The child was wet . . . the child did weep." These are the beads he
strings together to make the *Songs*. It is a world of plain identities, pro-
gressions, and contrasts. Only rarely does *Innocence* have a construction
even so complicated as "wrath by his meekness / And by his health.
sickness."

In *Experience*, which is a briefer group, only love, weep, and night
appear more than ten times, although variations of self, father, hand,
and fear follow close behind. *Experience* is slightly less mesmeric than
Innocence, less restricted. As befits its broader world, where the symbols can be more diverse, fewer terms repeat from song to song. Within
the poems there is still a fairly high degree of repetition, from "O Earth
O Earth" and "Tyger Tyger" to "The Human Dress . . . The Human
Form . . . The Human Face . . . The Human Heart." The rule of
parallel phrasing also still holds.

In brevity of sentence-structure, which is almost as significant a
feature of these songs as verbal repetition, the two groups are virtually
identical. The typical complete sentence time and again takes only one
or two lines:

> I have no name.   *(Innocence*, p. 118)

> And now beside thee bleating lamb
> I can lie down and sleep;   *(Innocence*, p. 119)

> O Rose thou art sick.   *(Experience*, p. 213)

> Am not I
> A fly like thee?   *(Experience*, p. 213)

> But a Pebble of the brook,
> Warbled out these metres meet.

> > *(Experience*, p. 211)

In longer sentences the common lengtheners are "and" and "but,"
"if" and "when." Clauses remain brief. As a result, the single unit
of the line almost becomes the unit of perception. The line is vivid,
compact, complete, a moment of vision; each song composed of such
lines is a chain of such moments; and each set of songs is constructed
like a mosaic out of these innumerable tiny independent parts.

The metrical form of the songs both reinforces these traits of diction and structure, and is reinforced by them. In both *Innocence* and *Experience* the stanzaic patterns are extremely plain. The lines are usually short, seldom longer than a tetrameter, so that the rhymes come thick and fast. The stanzas themselves are brief units, most commonly quatrains in couplets or cross-rhyme. Only one poem of *Innocence* is in pentameter, one in septenary, and one in dimeter quatrains with a single-line pentameter refrain. In *Experience,* only the "Introduction" and "Earth's Answer," less simple than the rest in diction and more abstract in theme, use complex stanzas. Except for the pentameter refrain of "A Little Girl Lost," no line in *Experience* is longer than four beats. The lines are almost invariably end-stopped in both books, and because the line-unit is also the unit of meaning, we are not allowed to leap ahead or to suspend our thought from line to line. Blake makes us take baby steps, and we feel that each line affords a finished, if minute, esthetic satisfaction.

The use of pause in these poems adds symmetry to simplicity. Consider one of Blake's most famous quatrains:

> Tyger Tyger. / burning bright
> In the forests / of the night;
> What immortal / hand or eye
> Could frame / thy fearful symmetry.

The first two lines each split roughly in half, with the same number of beats before and after the pause. The third line can really be read without a pause, but if there were a break, it would come after "immortal," again dividing the line down the middle. Only the fourth line is asymmetrical. The remainder of "The Tyger" contains only one other asymmetrical line. This pattern is the norm for the *Songs,* as in the following typical first lines from *Innocence:*

> Piping down / the valleys wild
>
> Once a dream / did weave a shade
>
> The Sun / does arise
>
> Sweet dreams / form a shade
>
> Twas on a Holy Thursday / their innocent faces clean,

or these from *Experience:*

> Love seeketh not / itself to please

A little black thing / among the snow

O Rose / thou art sick

Dear Mother, Dear Mother, / the Church is cold.

Lines of two or four feet either split evenly or do not split at all, with few exceptions. Only some of the more rhetorical pieces like "The Divine Image" and "On Another's Sorrow" in *Innocence*, "The Little Vagabond," "London," and "A Little Boy Lost" in *Experience*, have more than three asymmetrical lines. The three-beat poems usually omit the pause.

These stanza forms of three and four beats, symmetrically divided, are like nursery rhymes, folk songs, and ballads. The four-stress line divided into distichs, with alliteration to help the stresses, was also the meter of *Beowulf*. Although this line may or may not be in some mysterious way "native" to English,[3] it has historically acquired an aura of naturalness, primitiveness, and artlessness, at hand to any poet who uses it. Because of all these factors, we can intone Blake's songs with the kind of regular jingle or thump which children enjoy, without severe distortion. Most poetry cannot be read in this way. We cannot let our voices thump primitively through

Of *man's* first *disobe*dience *and* the *fruit*

True *wit* is *N*ature *to* ad*v*antage *dress'd*

That *time* of *year* thou *mayst* in *me* be*hold*

without feeling silly. But a primitively accented

*Lit*tle *Lamb* who *made* thee
Dost thou *know* who *made* thee

does not sound too foolish, even if, ordinarily, we might prefer to stress the "made" in each line a little less, and the first "who" more. And the primitive

*T*yger *T*yger. *bur*ning *bright,*
In the *forests* of the *night*

rings in our minds even when we do not intend to stress "in" and "of." Short lines are easier to accent regularly. Alliterated words are easier to accent strongly. A central pause emphasizes the accents. Parallel constructions, brief phrases, images without surface difficulty, all encourage

[3] See Northrop Frye, *Anatomy of Criticism* (Princeton, 1957), p. 251.

reading with a fixed beat. This is the first form of rhythm the human ear can perceive. It remains the most accessible, since it is associated with regular organic processes like heartbeat, with semivoluntary activities like breathing and walking, and with simple exercises like foot-tapping and hand-clapping. Blake's *Songs* are so constructed that we will hear in them, with a part of our ear, the unsophisticated succession of regular beats, even while our conscious reading accents more subtly. This undercurrent of simple rhythm must be allowed to go its way, affecting us kinetically rather than mentally, or we will miss a good part of Blake's message.

Yet we cannot ignore the superstructure Blake erects on his primitive rhythmical base. The drawback of children's songs is that they all sound rather alike, lacking the "minute particulars" which induce the more refined mental and emotional satisfactions in poetry. One lullaby, one comic jingle, one counting-out rhyme, is like another. The tune counts more than the words. This is not so in Blake's *Songs*.

To help him fit his measures to his meanings, Blake began with a command of more meters than were dreamt of in the current prosodic philosophy. Iambs, of course, were standard fare. Blake could never serve them up with proper Popean flourish, although some of the notebook epigrams aim at it. Usually he does not try. About a fourth of the lyrics in *Innocence*, and a third in *Experience*, are iambic. They are the soberer pieces in each book: "The Little Black Boy," "The Divine Image," "Holy Thursday" in *Innocence*, the didactic "London," "The Clod and the Pebble," "A Little Boy Lost" and "To Tirzah" in *Experience*. His accomplishment in the pentameter quatrain rivals that of Gray's *Elegy*. From such poems as "The Little Black Boy," remarks Damon, "it would be very difficult to know that Dryden and Pope had existed." [4]

The trochaic line, somewhat less popular in the eighteenth century, was a favorite of Blake's, from which he elicited diverse effects. Several of his best-known pieces are trochaic. One student of metrics finds this "the chief technical means by which Blake obtains his characteristic infantine effect, and gives the impression of speaking through the lips of a child," [5] as in "The Lamb," "The Blossom" or "The Little Girl Lost." This childlike effect comes from the fact that trochaic rhythms,

[4] S. Foster Damon, *William Blake: His Philosophy and Symbols* (Boston, 1924), p. 47. [A selection from this book is included among the essays in this volume.—Ed.]
[5] Enid Hamer, *The Metres of English Poetry* (London, 1930), p. 242.

since they start on the downbeat and are usually subject to less variation than iambs, give a more emphatic feeling. They have a quality
of directness which lends itself well to Blake's "infant" style. But "Love
and harmony combine" from *Poetical Sketches*, "The Tyger" and "A
Poison Tree" from *Experience*, and "Never seek to tell thy love" from
the Rossetti Notebook, are all different and all excellent. Between one-
half and one-third of the poems in *Innocence*, including many of the
longer ones, are trochaic; somewhat fewer in *Experience*.

Finally, the uses of anapestic meters, e.g., in "The Ecchoing Green,"
"The Chimney Sweeper," "The Shepherd," and "Laughing Song" in
Innocence alone, were virtually his own discovery.

Discussing Blake's anapests, Damon somewhat erroneously states that
the Elizabethans never used this meter except accidentally and with
poor results.[6] Exceptions, for example the finale of Jonson's "Celebration of Charis," do exist. And, although this was considered a low bur-
lesque meter in the neoclassical period, and was stigmatized as such by
Bysshe,[7] Damon errs in implying that the eighteenth century continued
to use anapest exclusively for "drinking songs and hunting choruses."
The meter was popularized by Prior for dainty society verse and used
by Shenstone for pastoral ballads and Cowper for "The Poplar Field."
Watts, out of his thousand poems, have five in anapest, and Wesley has
thousands of anapestic lines. Wesley, however, inclines to gallop:

> I rode on the Sky
> (Freely justified I!)
> Nor envied *Elijah* his Seat;
> My Soul mounted higher
> In a Chariot of Fire,
> And the Moon it was under my feet.

Thus although anapest was not unknown in Blake's time, the few
serious poems in this meter never exceed prettiness, and tend to lapse
into singsong.

Blake's handling of the meter avoids this hazard. We might have
expected him to produce poems like the dimpling

> The Sun does arise,
> And make happy the skies.

> (*Innocence*, p. 116)

---

[6] Damon, *Blake*, pp. 45–46.
[7] See pp. 16–17, *supra*.

When the voices of children are heard on the green
And laughing is heard on the hill,

(Innocence, p. 121)

for anapest is well suited to a cheerful, rapid run, in waltz or polka time. But he is not limited to such relatively obvious music. The anapest darkens, with him, to form the strangely grave beat of the first "Chimney Sweeper," the ironic spriteliness of "The Garden of Love," and the terrible, gyring "Rose thou art sick" of *Experience,* where the waltz has become a *danse macabre.*

The poet's facility with trochaic and anapestic measures permits him a greater range of expressiveness than confinement to iambs alone would allow. The iambic poems are closest to normal discursive or argumentative speech. The trochaic poems are barer, more emphatic, purer. The poems in anapest resemble music, and carry the reader along more by the swing and sway of rhythm than by any rational content. Blake had another advantage over his contemporaries: a willingness to vary his lines internally in a manner which had not been practised since the seventeeth century. These irregularities have the double function of avoiding metrical monotony, and of helping him realize his ideas and emotions with as much precision as possible.

The importance of variation in English metrics cannot be over-emphasized. If a poet has established enough of a regular metric pattern to set some beat going in our heads, the next most important thing for him is to know how to ring changes on it. These changes will form a counterpoint to the steady beat underneath, and the combination of base-beat and counterpoint will create the unique rhythm of a poem, which a reader always feels whether he knows what is happening or not, and will also help create its unique mood. One of the things that hindered eighteenth-century poets from achieving as full an emotional or musical range as their seventeenth-century forebears or nineteenth-century heirs was their inhibition about metrical irregularity.

To understand the quality of Blake's counterpoint, it will be useful to consider which techniques of variation he did not use, as well as those he did; and also to note where he went beyond the established techniques even of earlier times. The following list of standard variations in English metrics may therefore be compared with Blake's practice.

1. Foot-inversion: usually iamb ˘ ′ inverted to trochee ′ ˘. Inversion of the first foot in iambic meters was a variation common enough to pass uncensured by Augustan critics. Internal inversion was uncommon and

final-foot inversion was ignored or condemned by almost everyone, although Milton unquestionably uses it in several lines. A notable Romantic example is Keats' "Bright star! would I were steadfast as thóu ărt." In trochaic and other meters, inversion rarely occurs.

2. Foot-distention: use of more than one stress in a foot, as in a spondee ′ ′ . Eighteenth-century writers used spondees, though they may not have called them that; e.g., Pope's "Shút, shút the door, good John!"

3. Foot-substitution: use of a trisyllabic foot for a disyllable, or vice versa. Discovery of this "new" principle, generally ignored in the eighteenth century, was Coleridge's great announcement in the preface to *Christabel*. On the same principle is:

4. Incomplete or monosyllabic foot: a syllable is dropped, or pause takes the place of a syllable, as in music. The classic example is Tennyson's

> Break,　　break,　　break,
> On thy cold grey stones, O sea!

Not affecting the scansion as such, but also used to avoid monotonous cadence, are:

1. Enjambment: run-on or absence of pause at the close of the line.

2. Use of pause or caesura within the line: variation of its position.

3. Accentual variation: (a) light or omitted accent on a syllable in stress position—usually admissible anywhere but in the last foot, and sometimes occurring there also; (b) variations in degree of normal stress, indicated, from primary to secondary to tertiary, by ′, ˆ, `, in the notation currently used in American linguistics.[8] These distinctions, although not ordinarily perceived conciously by an untrained ear, help order the meaning of sentences to us.

4. Variations in tempo, produced partly by heaviness of accent and pause, partly by presence or absence of long vowels or diphthongs, liquidity or clustering of consonants.

[8] See George C. Trager and Henry Lee Smith, Jr., *An Outline of English Structure, Studies in Linguistics,* Occasional Papers, No. 3 (Norman, Okla., 1951).
　　Among the articles which have applied the Trager-Smith notation to prosody are: Harold Whitehall, "From Linguistics to Criticism"; Seymour Chatman, "Robert Frost's 'Mowing': an Inquiry into Prosodic Structure"; and Chatman, "Mr. Stein on Donne," all in the symposium "English Verse and What it Sounds Like," *Kenyon Review,* XVIII (1956), 411–77. These are more significant as propaganda than as analysis, and have provoked dissenting articles such as W. K. Wimsatt and Monroe C. Beardsley, "The Concept of Meter: an Exercise in Abstraction," *PMLA,* LXXIV (1959), 585–98.
　　Some more recent, and more genuinely analytical, articles which employ this notation are: Martin Halpern, "On the Two Chief Metrical Modes in English," *PMLA,* LXXVII (1962), 177–86 (in which "The Tyger" is analyzed, p. 179); Joseph M. Williams, "Caliban and Ariel Meet Trager and Smith," *CE,* XXIV (1962), 121–26; and Frederic G. Cassidy, "From Stress to Rhythm—Some Analytic Considerations," Unpubl. art. (Madison, 1962).

The variations of this second group, dependent as they are on the writer's habits of syntax, sentence-structure and sound-pattern, also depend on each reader's habits of intonation, on whether he prefers more or less stress, more or less pause at a given point. Thus, individual instances of such variation, when not bluntly dictated by syntax and punctuation, are often disputable. The general principle is not. Pope, being denied access to most of the major variations, had to rely on these minor ones. They, therefore, make all the difference between the elegant Leviathan of the eighteenth century, and the smaller fish who hurried in his wake. In Blake, however, the situation almost reverses itself, for he makes rather less use of the minor variations, and more of the major.

Only one of these minor variations finds no place in the *Songs of Innocence and Experience:* enjambment, with its verse-paragraph functions. Although Blake was experimenting with run-on in *Poetical Sketches,* and was already developing a paragraph technique in several Prophetic Books composed before the etching of *Experience,* the lyrics of both *Innocence* and *Experience* depend on chains of single lines linked by the conspicuous chime of like sounds; their music gives one grain of sand at a time, rather than the prospect of a whole beach at once. Thus the lines are almost always end-stopped.

Two other variations used only slightly in the *Songs* are asymmetrical pause-placement and dropped accents. As observed above, Blake's pauses tend to split his lines in half. In addition, he tends to avoid placing light syllables in stress positions. He does have some lines like:

I was angry wĭth my friend

(*Experience,* p. 218)

Gave thee clothing ŏf delight

(*Innocence,* p. 115)

Nor is it possiblĕ to Thought
A greater thăn Itself to know.

(*Experience,* p. 218)

But these are relatively rare. If there were many more, the verse would lose its steady thump.

Still, despite the sparseness of dropped accents and unbalanced pauses, the rhetoric provides enough slight variation to prevent monotony. The "Introduction" to *Innocence,* for example, remains lively despite its considerable regularity. This becomes clear if we use the notation of structural linguistics:

> Píping dówn the válleys wíld
> Píping sóngs of pléasant glée
> Òn a clóud I sâw a chíld.
> And hé láughing sáid to mê.
>
> Pípe a sóng abôut a Lámb:
> Sò I píped with mérry chéar,
> Píper pípe that sóng agáin—
> Sò I píped, he wépt to héar.

(Innocence, p. 111)

The tripping quality of this measure, and of many others in Blake, is due to our skimming past one or more full accents in over half the lines. Several of the stresses I have marked might be considered optional by a still more skim-minded reader; e.g., "down," l. 1, "song," l. 7. Conversely, one might wish to accent "saw," l. 3. Note also that the internal pause, where it exists, comes mostly after the third syllable, but once clearly after the fourth (l. 4), and once after the second (l. 7).

To illustrate the importance even of slight differences in degree of stress, perhaps the clearest example is the last stanza of "Spring," where the lines could hardly be shorter, the beat more regular, or the diction more monosyllabic. Almost no room remains for any variation; yet the verse simply does not read so rigidly as a strict scansion of it,

$$ \prime \smile \prime \;\mid\; \prime \smile \prime \;\mid\; \prime \smile \prime \;\mid\; \prime \smile \prime \;\mid\;, \text{etc.,} $$

would imply, for the degree of stress is not quite identical everywhere. My reading is as follows:

> Líttlĕ Lámb
> Hére Ĭ ám,
> Cóme ănd líck
> Mỳ whĭte néck.
> Lét mĕ pûll
> Yòur sŏft Wóol.
> Lét mĕ kîss
> Yòur sŏft fáce.
> Mérrĭlў Mérrĭlў, wĕ wélcŏme ín thĕ Yéar.

(Innocence, p. 123)

The tone would be a somewhat wheedling one: "*Come* and . . . *Let me* . . . *Let* me," changing into bouncing assurance for the dactyls and iambs of the refrain. Probably, too, some account should be made of the slight difference in rhythm between the disyllable "Little" and the monosyllables "Here I"; of the slight difference in length of pronunciation between "and . . . me . . . me" and "white . . . soft . . . soft" which gives the latter words a shade more emphasis; and of the differences in strength of the pauses at the line-ends. Put together, all these variations produce even in this least complex of poetic constructions a little play of contrapuntal pattern: while the rhyme-scheme gives the pattern aa bb cc dd e, the rhetorical structure of the phrases gives a pattern 1,2 3,4 3,4 3,4 5.

Blake's control of tempo may be seen if we compare certain poems with each other. The line of "Little Lamb who made thee" is slower than "Merry Merry Sparrow," although they scan alike. A few of the lyrics also reveal some internal variation of tempo. In "London," for example, the first stanza has a moderate pace:

> I wander thro' each charter'd street,
> Near where the charter'd Thames does flow
> And mark in every face I meet
> Marks of weakness, marks of woe.

> (*Experience,* p. 216)

Then, in its progress of vision from the surface stigmata, "marks," of evil to the internal causes, "mind-forg'd manacles," and finally to perception of the inevitable connections between evils, "London" reads in a crescendo of volume, intensity, and sonorousness, growing slower and more damning at each stage, until the final

> But most thro' midnight streets I hear
> How the youthful Harlots curse
> Blasts the new born Infants tear,
> And blights with plagues the Marriage hearse

with its strong alliteration, the explosive consonant clusters of *"blasts . . . blights . . . plagues"* and, to cap "Harlots curse," the bitterly outflung "Marriage hearse."

"The Fly" shifts tempo in mid-course. The opening is rather rapid, rather conspicuously casual:

> Little Fly
> Thy summers play,
> My thoughtless hand
> Has brush'd away.

> (*Experience,* p. 213)

Succeeding stanzas keep this tone, up to the easy homiletic "For I dance / and drink and sing / Till some blind hand / Shall touch my wing." This is ancient doctrine: Blake has said nothing new yet. Then in the fourth stanza comes the change:

> If thought is life
> And strength & breath;
> And the want
> Of thought is death;

The language is suddenly impersonal, the idea striking, and the words more difficult to articulate because of the consonants. We are forced to slow up, to pronounce each key word deliberately: "if thought—is life—and strength—and breath. . . ." But in the last stanza the poem returns to its initial smiling rapidity. "Then am I / A happy fly. / If I live / or if I die." "The Fly" has been considered a hard poem to understand, among critics who try to expound Blake's meanings logically.[9] This is because the façade of logic in the poem is a joke, a trap. If we listen without ratiocination to the poem's sound, we find a dialectic of moods from tarnished cheerfulness, to solemnity, to a higher cheerfulness, which is not at all effected by logical means. The conclusion of Blake's if-then construction does not *follow* from its premise, although both premise and conclusion are assumed true. What happens instead is that the poet is momentarily lifted from the plane of moral reflection to the plane of vision. He discovers himself thinking —with sudden fervor—that "thought is life," and realizes by his own intensity of thought that he himself is alive, and therefore happy, and therefore like the fly (which of course also thinks and is happy), and that nothing else matters. It does not even matter if he will die in the future, since he has discovered himself living now. The last stanza can afford to be purely merry, because Blake's moment of vision has obliterated both his guilt about the fly and his concern for his own morrow.

In the original MS version of this poem, the final stanza came immediately after the third: "For I dance / And drink & sing / . . . Then am I / A happy fly." This makes sense, but lacks power. It leaves the

[9] See the controversy in *Essays in Criticism*, XI (1961): Leo Kirschbaum, "Blake's 'The Fly,'" pp. 154–62; F. W. Bateson, "An Editorial Postscript," pp. 162–63; and John E. Grant, "Misreadings of 'The Fly,'" pp. 481–86. Robert Gleckner, *The Piper and the Bard* (Detroit, 1959), p. ix, has declared that he does not know how to read this poem. [An extract from Mr. Gleckner's book is included among the selections in this volume.—Ed.]

poem all on one level. By inserting the crucial fourth stanza, Blake spoiled his logic and perfected his lyric. "The Fly" is an excellent example of a poem which achieves its ends through surface manipulation.

Except in "London" and "The Fly," internal tempo-variation is an insignificant part of Blake's technique. This is not surprising, since most of the songs express stasis rather than progress; they keep to one pace for the same reason that they keep their lines end-stopped.

In his use of the minor variations, Blake does no more than any competent lyricist might do. Except for small signs like the single-stanza break in tone and tempo of "The Fly," which would never have been perpetrated by a Collins or Gray, it is difficult to distinguish him, technically, from other poets of his age. Only in the major variations, where formal scansion is affected and where his contemporaries feared to tread too far, does his difference become pronounced.

Inversion, the most commonly acknowledged of the major variations, figures in thirteen of the 23 songs in *Innocence,* fifteen of the 23 (counting "A Divine Image") in *Experience.* Most of the usages are initial, although internal inversion, as in

> When the painted birds láugh ĭn the shade,
>
> *(Innocence,* p. 125)

occurs occasionally in both books. Blake does not invert his iambs very heavily compared with other poets. But he does break precedent by having several inverted trochees, sometimes bearing considerable expressive weight. In "Earth's Answer," an inverted initial foot throws stress on the phrase "frée Lóve":

> Selfish! vain!
> Eternal bane!
> Thăt frée Love with bondage bound.
>
> *(Experience,* p. 211)

In "On Another's Sorrow," the repeated cry "And not" throws stress on "not"; it is a lyric of incredulity:

> Can I see anothers woe,
> Ănd nót be in sorrow too.
> Can I see anothers grief,
> Ănd nót seek for kind relief.
>
> *(Innocence,* p. 122)

In "The Tyger," two inversions in one line emphasize the mystery-denoting particle "what":

> Ănd whát shoulder, & whát art,
> Could twist the sinews of thy heart?
>
> *(Experience,* p. 214)

In each case, the suggestion of a human voice, articulating its anger, wonder, or terror, is the more vivid because of the wrenched accents.

Like initial iambic inversions, spondaic feet were accepted among Blake's peers. In the *Songs,* spondees appear fairly frequently, usually for some specific rhetorical emphasis, as in "Súch súch were the joys" or "The mínd-|fórg'd mán|acles I hear." They can also help mold the entire spirit of a poem, when tellingly employed as in "The Tyger," where they pound away repeatedly, or in the two flower lyrics of *Experience,* "O Rose thou art sick" and "The Sunflower":

> Áh Sún-flower! weary of time.
> Who countest the steps of the Sun:
>
> *(Experience,* p. 215)

This tragically top-heavy effect in the opening, with the slender stem-like regularity of the remainder of the poem, anticipates Tennyson's

> Heavily hangs the broad sunflower
> Over its grave i' the earth so chilly.

Or there is that poised effect produced by the final spondee in a tiny Notebook lyric:

> He who binds to himself a joy[10]
> Does the winged life destroy;
> But he who kisses the joy as it flies
> Lives in eternity's sún ríse.
>
> *(Notebook,* p. 179)

Blake also, I think uniquely among English poets except Browning, sometimes slips extra stresses in among his anapests, generating quite novel rhythms. He does this a few times in the first "Chimney Sweeper," where he lets the speaker's enthusiasm overflow into extra accents for an effect of wide-eyed eagerness:

---

[10] Keynes' reading is "bends"; Joseph H. Wicksteed, *Blake's Innocence and Experience* (London, Toronto, and New York, 1928), p. 271 n., claims to see a dot over the vowel, and reads "binds." The latter word is more typical of Blake.

That thousands of sweepĕrs Díck Jóe, | Néd ӗ̆ Jáck

And by came an Angel who had ӑ́ bríght kéy

Then down a green plain léapĭng láughing, they run.

(Innocence, p. 117)

Quite a different effect appears at the close of "The Ecchoing Green."
The first two stanzas here end with a merry refrain: "While our sports
shall be seen / On the Ecchoing Green." "In our youth time were
seen / On the Ecchoing Green." But the third, which tells of sunset
and twilight after the day of mirth, when the children are gathered
to their mothers, concludes gravely:

And sport nó móre seen
On the darkening Green.

(Innocence, p. 116)

Monosyllabic feet are rare in Blake, as in most English verse. Two
notable instances, however, occur in the swaying rhythms of "A
Cradle Song," and in the powerful first line of the "Introduction" to
Experience:

Héar | thĕ vóice | ŏf thĕ Bárd!

where the successive feet consist of one, two, and three syllables.

This brings us to the technique of substitution, which is milk to
modern taste, but was bones to the critical philosophy of Blake's day.
Blake had begun substituting anapests for iambs in several of the
Poetical Sketches, most radical of which was the "Mad Song." Slightly
over half the lyrics of both *Innocence* and *Experience* are sown with
substitution, and the gain in flexible movement seems incalculable.
Blake's use of this device marks his emancipation from the golden cage
of eighteenth-century precept. He could also use his versatility to create
new patterns in which a particular variation becomes the rule, and
freedom is turned to the service of order. One charming instance of
such patterning is the mixed-meter stanza of "Laughing Song," with
its iambic catches among the anapests:

When the green woods laugh with the voice of joy
And the dimpling stream runs laughing by,
When the air does laugh with our merry wit.
And the green hill laughs with the noise of it.

(Innocence, p. 124)

Another is "Night," which has a stanzaic pattern consisting of a ballad quatrain followed by four lines in anapestic dimeter. In each stanza, the iambic lines are placed as it were horizontally, with independent clauses which parallel each other, while the anapests, in a soft continuous flow of one sentence, suggest the vertical:

> The sun descending in the west,
> The evening star does shine.
> The birds are silent in their nest,
> And I must seek for mine.
> The moon like a flower,
> In heavens high bower;
> With silent delight,
> Sits and smiles on the night.

(Innocence, p. 118)

The repeated alternation from stanza to stanza produces a sensation of hovering between waking and dream.

A third instance is "The Sick Rose," which gives the impression of strictest unity where Blake is in fact being most free. In my reading, only the fourth and eighth lines scan identically:

> Ó Róse thŏu ărt síck.
> Thĕ ĭnvísĭblĕ wórm.
> Thăt flíes ĭn thĕ níght
> Ĭn thĕ hówlĭng stórm:
>
> Hăs fóund óut thȳ béd
> Ŏf crímsŏn jóy:
> Ănd hĭs dárk sécrĕt lóve
> Dŏes thȳ lífe dĕstróy.

(Experience, p. 213)

When read without pauses, this approaches the pulse of continuous anapest. The downward, spiraling motion fits the poem's evocation of eroticism. The sound-linked spondees *ó Róse, Fóund óut, dárk sécret,* make the motion slow, emphatic, and therefore the more cruel. The anapests, and the sound-links between accents—*síck, invísible; flíes, níght; in the níght / In the hówling; hówling, fóund óut; lóve / Does thy lífe*—give the sense of inevitability. The effect is a fierce one, which the balancing iambs and spondees on either side of the anapests punctuate without dissipating. Nor was this a first fine careless rapture. The closing lines of Blake's original draft, "O dark secret love / Doth life destroy," with only two fewer anapests, are much weaker.

These poems illustrate what is perhaps most characteristically Blakean in the metric of the *Songs,* their repeated use of mixed measures. About one-third of the *Songs* are in mixed iamb-anapest meters; some like "The Sick Rose" and "Laughing Song" combining the two kinds of feet in almost every line, a few like "Night" juxtaposing whole lines of each. Another third mix iambic and trochaic lines, usually with the trochees dominating, for one of Blake's favorite devices was to relieve a too insistent trochaic beat with an occasional iambic line. In "The Little Girl Lost" and "The Little Girl Found," the few iambic lines enhance Blake's studied effect of naïveté. It is as if the lisper of these poems could not manage to keep straight even so simple a pattern as the trochaic trimeter. In "A Poison Tree," however, there is deliberate drama. After the situation of suppressed wrath against a foe has been established in the first stanza, succeeding stanzas erect a kind of grisly mockery of the tune in the "Introduction" to *Innocence.* There the tune was of free creativity, here it is of perverse creativity, the nourishment of hate's poison tree: "Ând Ĭ wátĕrd . . . Ând Ĭ súnnĕd . . . Ând ĭt gréw . . . Ând mў fóe. . . ." It is all in trochaics, until the last line; but then the relief of tension, the relaxation from trochees to an iambic line, is the relief of death:

> And into my garden stole.
> When the night had veild the pole;
> In the morning glad I see;
> My foe outstretchd beneath the tree.

> *(Experience,* p. 218)

A final example of how Blake employed mixed meters for expressive ends is "The Tyger," where an iambic line serves at several points like a water boy among the hammering trochees and spondees. The first stanza is preparation:

> Tyger Tyger. burning bright,
> In the forests of the night;
> What immortal hand or eye,
> Could frame thy fearful symmetry?

> *(Experience,* p. 214)

The final iambic line here provides a break, or breath, preventing the poem from building up too rapidly. The second stanza is entirely trochaic. The third stanza sandwiches two regular iambic lines between the trochaic-spondaic ones:

Ǎnd whát shóuldĕr, & whát árt,
Cŏuld twíst thĕ sínĕws ŏf thў héart?
Ǎnd whén thў héart bĕgán tŏ béat,
Whát dréad hánd? & whát dréad féet?

Here there is already something insinuating and ominous in the iambic
lines. The fourth stanza, in which the creation of the Tyger culminates,
is again all pounding trochees. The fifth, quieter and more fearsome,
is again half-and-half:

Did he smile his work to see?
Did he who made the Lamb make thee?

Note how the accents shifts: first "Díd hĕ," then "Díd hé." *Did he?*
And the final stanza, answering nothing, returns to the opening—with
a difference:

Tyger Tyger. burning bright,
In the forests of the night;
What immortal hand or eye,
Dáre fráme thy fearful symmetry?

It is no longer a matter of "Could frame," the phrase of physical might,
but "Dare frame." In closing his fearfully symmetrical circle, Blake
opens the question of moral power. The longer vowel, and the sound-
link of the *r*'s, make us dwell on this spondee which has replaced the
first stanza's iamb. It is only a slight touch; but it completes the poem.

T. S. Eliot has paid Blake a high compliment by finding in him
"merely a peculiar honesty, which, in a world too frightened to be
honest, is peculiarly terrifying. It is an honesty against which the whole
world conspires, because it is unpleasant. . . . And this honesty never
exists without great technical accomplishment." [11] The technical accomplishment of Blake's candid lyrics involved a double temerity. In
the first place, he dared to write serious poetry with the basic rhythmical and linguistic tools of a prattling child. In the second, he dared
to think thoughts and hear melodies whose precise expression required
breaking some universally accepted metrical conventions. The latter
achievement, which it is easy for the lens of prosodic history to magnify,
should not obscure the former, which was at least an essential to
Blake's lyric gift. They dovetail, one defining the particulars of
emotion and idea, the other the generalities of simplicity and purity.

[11] T. S. Eliot, *The Sacred Wood* (London, 1934), p. 151.

Probably Blake did not realize the extent of his boldness, for his "peculiar honesty" kept company with a peculiar oblivion to certain things in the world about him. His friend Cunningham wrote that Blake at the outset of his career "thought that he had but to sing songs and draw designs, and become great and famous." [12] To be sure, he knew that he was not writing like Pope or Dr. Johnson; but did he know that he was writing like no one else? His acquaintance was artistic, not literary. He would hardly have paid attention to the finer points of contemporary prosodic faith, and perhaps not even to some of the cruder ones, despite owning a copy of Bysshe.[13]

The Blake of *Innocence* and *Experience* is like a choirboy in the back row singing sweet and sour songs to please himself, unaware of what the rest of the chorus is doing. He differs more by inadvertence than by conscious rebellion. In the Prophetic Books, the case is altered to deliberate rebellion. Before considering the technique of the Prophetic Books, however, it will be necessary to discuss the other half of Blake's lyric music, its vowel and consonant patterns; and also to review the later lyrics, which deviate in both ends and means from *Innocence* and *Experience*.

[12] Allan Cunningham, *Life of Blake,* in Arthur Symons, *William Blake* (New York, 1907), p. 401.

[13] It is likely that Blake worked by ear, not by rule, but we cannot be sure of this. Notwithstanding his inclinations to expound, sometimes at tedious and cranky length, his theories and practices in the visual arts, we have from him only the barest, most equivocal clues about his poetic methods. Perhaps one reason for this is that, considering himself a professional artist rather than a professional poet, he did not feel so much called upon to enter the lists of self-defense, or to spend time on intramural squabbles, in the field of poetry. Thus he may have developed a theory or theories of prosody comparable to his theory of outline in drawing and painting, but not written on it. It seems more plausible, however, that he felt words did not require explanations, even to himself, in the same way pictures did; and that the spirits that guided his hand, and of whom he dared not "pretend to be any other than the Secretary" (*Letters*, p. 825), simply kept their own counsel.

The Initial Eden

by S. Foster Damon

The corn was orient and immortal wheat, which never should be reaped, nor was ever sown. I thought it had stood from everlasting to everlasting. The dust and stones of the street were as precious as gold: the gates were at first the end of the world. The green trees when I saw them first through one of the gates transported and ravished me, their sweetness and unusual beauty made my heart to leap, and almost mad with ecstasy, they were such strange and wonderful things. The Men! O what venerable and reverend creatures did the aged seem! Immortal Cherubims! And young men glittering and sparkling Angels, and maids strange seraphic pieces of life and beauty! Boys and girls tumbling in the street, and playing, were moving jewels. I knew not that they were born or should die; But all things abided eternally as they were in their proper places. Eternity was manifest in the Light of the Day, and something infinite behind everything appeared: which talked with my expectation and moved my desire. The city appeared to stand in Eden, or to be built in Heaven. The streets were mine, and so were the sun and moon and stars, and all the world was mine; and I the only spectator and enjoyer of it. I knew no churlish proprieties nor bounds, nor divisions: but all proprieties and divisions were mine: all treasures and the possessors of them. So that with much ado I was corrupted and made to learn the dirty devices of this world. Which I now unlearn, and become, as it were, a little child again that I may enter into the Kingdom of God.

—THOMAS TRAHERNE
Centuries of Meditations, iii. 3.

The *Songs of Innocence* was the first great fruit of Blake's first mystical insight. The Mystic Way begins in the Garden of Eden. Blake

"The Initial Eden" by S. Foster Damon. From William Blake: His Philosophy and Symbols *(Boston: Houghton Mifflin, 1924), pp. 39–42. Reprinted by permission of Constable Publishers, London.*

identified at once the ecstasy of the revelation with the state of mind of a child, believing deeply that "of such are the Kingdom of Heaven." All of us can recollect the time when every common sight seemed "apparell'd in celestial light, the glory and the freshness of a dream"; when our feet were never tired of investigating the mysteries that lay beyond each rise of meadowland; and when we were intimate, as we never can be again, with every bend of the brooks for miles around. Then we accepted the world without suspicion of its troubles. What sorrows came to us disturbed only the surface of things, and passed away "like little ripples down a sunny river."

In just the same way the world seems entirely simple and happy to the newly initiated mystic. Intuition tells him all things; he reasons little more than does a child. Innocence is free, as it needs no laws. It is happy, since it is unsophisticated. It enjoys the most spontaneous communion with nature, readily perceiving the divine in all things. When trouble comes to others, it is ready with the completest sympathy, though without understanding. Its own sufferings are felt to be only temporary; they will be followed by some still greater happiness. All help each other, as the glowworm lights the lost ant home; and even when the wolves break in on the sheep, the lions are there to guard the slain lambs in the immortal home. Our bodies are a brief cloud, a coffin which an angel will soon unlock. The only God is Christ, the kind father, to whom children were always dearest. It is the Golden Age.

This Christian Arcadia is not limited to childhood. Any person who has not undergone an embittering contact with the world is yet innocent. Blake seems to have conceived the state of Innocence as ending generally with the passing of youth. Thel is still in the state of Innocence; and many of Blake's shepherds seem aged (if we dare age such immortal beings!) about eighteen. Job, Blake's extreme example, was an old man before his Experience came.

Thomas Traherne of the preceding century was perhaps the only other mystic who celebrated Innocence with Blake's enthusiasm. Having once appreciated it, he devoted the rest of his life to recapturing the first rapture, whose technical name, for him, was "Felicity." What it meant to him may be surmised from the following quotation:

> All appeared new and strange, at first, inexpressibly rare and delightful and beautiful. I was a little stranger, which at my entrance into the world was saluted and surrounded with innumerable joys. My knowledge was Divine. I knew by intuition those things which, since my Apostasy,

I collected again by the highest reason. My very ignorance was advantageous. I seemed as one brought into the Estate of Innocence.[1] All things were spotless and pure and glorious: yea, and infinitely mine, and joyful and precious. I knew not that there were any sins, or complaints or laws. I dreamed not of poverties, contentions, or vices. All tears and quarrels were hidden from mine eyes. Everything was at rest, free and immortal. I knew nothing of sickness or death or rents or exaction, either for tribute or bread. In the absence of these I was entertained like an Angel with the works of God in their splendour and glory. I saw all in the peace of Eden; Heaven and Earth did sing my Creator's praises, and could not make more melody to Adam than to me. All Time was Eternity and a perpetual Sabbath. Is it not strange, that an infant should be heir of the whole world, and see those mysteries which the books of the learned never unfold?

St. Francis also remains as one of the supreme examples of the state of Innocence, though he was also much more. Wordsworth's most famous Ode was only a lament that the state is lost so early.

Innocence, Heaven though it be, is not perfect. The child contains seeds of error, which must grow until they can be weeded out. "Man is born a Spectre or Satan," Blake wrote in his *Jerusalem* (52). "To be an Error and to be cast out is part of God's design," he explained still further in his *Last Judgment*. So Thel, ignorant of the world, is drawn irresistibly from her Eden. For, after all, Ignorance is not a means of Salvation; "the fool shall not enter into heaven, let him be ever so holy." [2] But Innocence knows nothing of this; and such thoughts do not appear in this first volume of *Songs*.

Yet there is one hint that Innocence is not everything. In the introductory poem, the Piper pipes his song about the Lamb twice: and the second time the Poetic Genius "wept to hear." Blake meant to indicate that Innocence had its "Contrary State," which later he was to call "Experience."

Blake, then, in writing about Innocence, was describing a mystical state, rather than childhood; but he identifies the two so closely that his poems seem to be spoken by the very children themselves. He does not contemplate children, in the manner of Wordsworth, Hugo, and Longfellow; he actually enters into their souls and speaks through

[1] Thomas Traherne, *Centuries of Meditations,* iii. 2. All mystics speak the same language. Blake could not have seen this passage, for Traherne died eighty-three years before Blake's birth, and his mystical works were not published until the present century.

[2] *Last Judgment (MS. Book).*

their own mouths. Only Stevenson repeated the feat; and even his children are conscious and prim beside Blake's. Blake's poems illustrate his own line in *Milton* (30): "How wide the Gulf & Unpassable! between Simplicity & Insipidity." For Blake is sweet without being sentimental, graceful without being weak, moral without being didactic, simple without being obvious. He dared the worst failures—those of triviality and affectation; and yet he always avoided them as completely as though they did not exist.

The *Songs of Innocence* are generally recognized as Blake's highest achievement as poet. A great deal of this opinion is due to the obscurity which increasingly overwhelms one in all his later work. Everybody can understand Innocence; but we do not willingly admit the facts of Experience; while the remote world of mystical knowledge is beyond the comprehension of most of us. Moreover, Blake's technical experiments in his later books tend to make many readers uneasy. But whether or not this is his most perfect work, it is unquestionably one of the most perfectly beautiful books of the world.

When Blake found himself at last, all the influences of other writers seemed to vanish. Both thought and form are completely his own. Watts is the only author we can positively name whose writings may have affected these *Songs* even slightly. Strictly speaking, Blake has even turned from the immediate future of the literary world; for he is now thoroughly a Mystic, rather than a Romanticist. The whole external world, whether literary or historical, had vanished, or left but the dimmest traces. Who could imagine from Blake's book that the French Revolution was then roaring its way into every one's soul?

But there were two general literary influences which deserve attention.

The Pastoral had always been one of the great traditions of English verse. From the days of the Elizabethans, it had passed through *Lycidas*, and was to reappear in such a masterpiece as *Adonais*. In the eighteenth century the pastoral had become almost wholly a matter of affectation. Hogarth had expelled it from painting, but the other arts still preserved it. Good old *Mother Goose* thus satirized the popular taste:

> Dear Sensibility, O la!
> I heard a little lamb cry, baa!
> Says I, "So you have lost mamma?"
>   "Ah!"

The little lamb, as I said so,
Frisking about the fields did go,
And, frisking, trod upon my toe.
                "Oh!"

Blake gave the tradition an entirely new turn. He employed all the pastoral properties as symbols of Innocence, and cast a mystical aura over the landscape. The result was that he made the pastoral something completely his own; infused it with artlessness and freshness—with spontaneity, in short—which completely differentiated his work from both that of his predecessors and his followers. It was as though a Fra Angelico, under the influence of St. Francis, had written poetry at the dictation of children; yet this does not wholly describe Blake's verses, for through them all blow the clear winds of April.

The second literary influence upon the *Songs* is more doubtful. Was Blake, in writing his poems of children, affected by their books? At the moment a new interest in the literature for children was already producing excellent results. The public was reacting from the hell-fire tales, the books of martyrs, and the like, which had been the usual reading given to children; and they found even Bunyan's absurd *Divine Emblems* not wholly appealing. So a new literature was springing up, which already included such immortals as *Mother Goose, Goody Two-Shoes,* and *Sanford and Merton.* Perrault's tales were translated, and old English legends were being revived from their chap-book existence. John Newbery won his niche in fame by giving these books a decent form: good English, good printing, good woodcuts, and unforgettable Dutch paper-covers. All these books (with the one exception of *Mother Goose*) were still primarily moralistic, but they had wholly cast away the morbid elements of the earlier books. The children had to wait for the great Victorians before they could read wholly unmoral books, like *Alice in Wonderland* and Edward Lear's *Nonsense Book.*

The *Songs of Innocence* must have been influenced at least slightly by this new spirit in children's books. Blake sustained the same moral tone in just the same way as his contemporaries, though it is subdued to a minimum. But the question goes farther than that: was Blake's own ear responsible for his original and instinctive cadences (which were quite unlike anything in the poetry of his day), or was he imitating the queer, yet satisfactory, metres of *Mother Goose?* Already in *An Island in the Moon* Blake had quoted *The Froggy would awooing ride;* and in the *Jerusalem* (of all places!) we find an unmistakable reminiscence of *Fa, fe, fi, fo, fum!*

> Boys and girls, come out to play,
> The moon does shine as bright as day

is strangely parallel in spirit to the *Nurse's Song.* Certainly, nothing in Blake's day approaches his *Songs* metrically, except *Mother Goose.*

But we can find neither real predecessors nor imitators. The *Songs of Innocence* remains one of the unique, inimitable achievements in books, whether it be considered from the poet's or the painter's standpoint. And the miracle seems the greater when we remember that Blake was always childless.

The Vision of Innocence

by Martin Price

William Blake's *Songs of Innocence* were engraved by 1789. Not until five years later were they incorporated into *The Songs of Innocence and Experience, Shewing the Two Contrary States of the Human Soul.* Partly because the *Songs of Innocence* have found their way into the nursery, partly because the *Songs of Experience* include some of Blake's most brilliant poems, there has been a tendency to discount the *Songs of Innocence* or to save them by reading them as highly ironic poems, each with its own built-in contraries. This produces strained readings and obscures the full import of Innocence as one of the "two contrary states." We must first take the *Songs of Innocence* in their own right, and by doing so we can make better sense of the *Songs of Experience.*

What the contrary states mean is shown in two poems Blake enclosed in letters to his friend and patron, Thomas Butts, the first on 2 October 1800, the second two years later, on 22 November 1802.[1] In the first the themes of Innocence are restated in the language of vision. Blake achieves an ecstatic transcendence on the shore at Felpham and looks down upon his mortal Shadow and his wife's. His eyes "Like a Sea without shore / Continue Expanding, / The Heavens

"The Vision of Innocence" by Martin Price. From To the Palace of Wisdom: Studies in Order and Energy from Dryden to Blake *(New York: Doubleday, 1964), pp. 389–401. Copyright © 1964, by Martin Price. Reprinted by permission of Doubleday & Company, Inc.*

[1] Quotations are cited from Geoffrey Keynes' edition of the *Complete Writings of William Blake*, London, 1957. They are identified by line number; by plate and line number for longer engraved poems; by page number for prose; by date for letters. Of the works on Blake, I am indebted chiefly to M. O. Percival, *William Blake's Circle of Destiny*, New York, 1938; Northrop Frye, *Fearful Symmetry*, Princeton, 1947; Stanley Gardner, *Infinity on the Anvil*, Oxford, 1954; Robert F. Gleckner, *The Piper & the Bard*, Detroit, 1959; Peter Fisher, *The Valley of Vision*, Toronto, 1961; and to Harold Bloom, for discussion and criticism, and for his writing on Blake, now summed up in *Blake's Apocalypse*, New York, 1963, which he allowed me to read in manuscript.

commanding." All Heaven becomes one man, Jesus, who purges away "All my mire & my clay" (as in "The Little Black Boy" or "The Chimney Sweeper") and enfolds Blake in his bosom, saying:

> This is My Fold,
> O thou Ram horn'd with gold,
> Who awakest from Sleep
> On the Sides of the Deep.

The lion and the wolf, whose "roarings resound," the "loud Sea & deep gulf"—all of them threatening—now become, for Jesus, "guards of My Fold."

> And the voice faded mild.
> I remain'd as a Child;
> All I ever had known
> Before me bright Shone.

This draws together visionary perception and childlike innocence, and makes visionary transcendence a discovery of the protected world of the divine sheepfold, where seeming evil is absorbed into a pastoral version of Order.

In the second of these poems we encounter the trials of Experience. Blake is torn with conflicting obligations; "the duties of life each other cross."

> Must Flaxman look upon me as wild,
> And all my friends be with doubts beguil'd?

Blake resolves the conflict by defying the sun and looking through its earthly form:

> Another Sun feeds our life's streams,
> We are not warmed with thy beams . . .
> My Mind is not with thy light array'd,
> Thy terrors shall not make me afraid.

The defiance makes all the natural world shrink and grieve, but Blake moves forward with triumph into the world of vision:

> The Sun was hot
> With the bows of my Mind & the Arrows of Thought—
> My bowstring fierce with Ardour breathes,
> My arrows glow in their golden sheaves.

"Now," he concludes, "I a fourfold vision see . . . Tis fourfold in my supreme delight." He has wrested vision from grief, and won through to a trust in his powers (pp. 816–18).

The *Songs of Innocence* cultivate a tone of naïvety, but we must recognize that what is spontaneously discovered by the child has in fact been earned by the poet's visionary powers. It is not easy to achieve Innocence, and one does not reach it by a simple process of subtraction. While the *Songs of Innocence* insist upon the naïve vision, they show, in their own way, as much calculation as the more radical of Wordsworth's *Lyrical Ballads*. Wordsworth's subjects are children, displaced persons or wanderers; humble people who live in dwellings all but indistinguishable from nature; morally displaced persons such as criminals and idiots—those rejected or oppressed by society; poets as social misfits and dreamers; and, most generally, people who have not entered and for some reason have fallen out of the social pattern. Wordsworth's treatment of them is a bold assertion of the dignity of their elementary feelings. Coleridge speaks of the "daring humbleness" of Wordsworth's language and versification, and we know that their challenge was felt and resisted by early critics. Blake's *Songs of Innocence* are more traditional in their literary and religious associations and more remote from such stubborn commonplaces of life as swelling ankles, idiot sons, and the love of property. But, like Wordsworth's poems, and, in fact, like most pastorals, they create a vision that risks one-sidedness. Such a vision teeters on the verge of calling to mind all it excludes, and Blake has given us what Innocence excludes in the *Songs of Experience*. But pastoral can teeter without falling into overt irony, and its assertion is all the more defiant for that poise.

The defiance is the poet's. The innocents themselves remain indifferent to all that crowds in upon us. This indifference is not ignorance, any more than it is in Wordsworth's "We Are Seven," where the child insists that her dead brother and sister are still in the midst of their family. The childlike trust becomes a metaphor for the more strenuous faith and defiance of doubt that all may achieve.

The landscape of Innocence is a fostering, humanized landscape. It echoes human songs and laughter; it accepts and sympathizes with every feeling. The "Laughing Song" is one of the simplest of the *Songs*, but Wordsworth found it worth copying into his commonplace book in 1804. It closes with the invitation to participate:

> When the painted birds laugh in the shade,
> Where our table with cherries and nuts is spread,

> Come live & be merry, and join with me,
> To sing the sweet chorus of "Ha, Ha, He."

The language is somewhat archaic ("painted birds"), the form reminiscent of Elizabethan lyrics, and the poem closes tellingly with the call to "sing the sweet chorus." The harmony of shepherds (the song first appears written in a copy of *Poetical Sketches* as *Sung . . . by a Young Shepherd*) and maids, of man and nature, is caught in the very meaningless exultation of the "Ha, Ha, He." If one calls it witless exultation, one has only underlined the point: this is the least self-conscious of sounds, the pure merry note. So it is with "Spring." Animal sounds, "infant noise," and the sounding flute are all part of one song; and child and lamb play together with no sense of difference. Music is only one manifestation of the reciprocal warmth that marks all relationships (every creature is related to every other); the nurse is trustful and indulgent, old John on the echoing green participates in the laughter of the children at play. There is neither jealousy nor restriction; darkness brings safe repose and satiation. The "happy Blossom" welcomes both the merry sparrow and the sobbing robin, rejoicing in its power to accept or comfort each alike.

In "The Lamb," the harmony grows out of a deeper union:

> I a child, & thou a lamb,
> We are called by his name.

Each creature is a member one of another because of their common membership in God's love and the body of His creation. This participation in one life is nicely stated in "The Shepherd," where the freedom of the shepherd ("From the morn to the evening he strays") is consonant with his watchfulness, for he is himself a sheep watched over by his Shepherd with generous love. The condition of peace is security without restraint. The participation is extended in "The Divine Image" to "every man of every clime," for every man—"heathen, turk, or jew"—is "Man, his child and care."

In "Night" all these themes come together. The moon sits in "heaven's high bower" like the happy blossom. The darkening fields are left by sleeping lambs to the "feet of angels bright." As in *Paradise Lost,*

> Millions of spiritual Creatures walk the Earth
> Unseen, both when we wake, and when we sleep
>   . . . oft in bands

While they keep watch, a nightly rounding walk
With Heav'nly touch of instrumental sounds
In full harmonic number join'd, their songs
Divide the night, and lift our thoughts to Heaven.

(IV, 677–78, 684–88)

Blake's world of Innocence is not, however, Paradise. The angels cannot always control wolves and tigers, or deny them victims; but the victims are received, "New worlds to inherit."

And there the lion's ruddy eyes
Shall flow with tears of gold,
And pitying the tender cries,
And walking round the fold,
Saying "Wrath, by his meekness,
And by his health, sickness
Is driven away
From our immortal day.

And now beside thee, bleating lamb,
I can lie down and sleep;
Or think on him who bore thy name,
Graze after thee and weep.
For, wash'd in life's river,
My bright mane for ever
Shall shine like the gold
As I guard o'er the fold."

(33–48)

The regeneration of the lion, so that he can now "remain always in Paradise," is a perhaps unconscious but eloquent reply to Mandeville's comment on Milton. . . . As the angels pitied the howling wolves and tigers, the lion can now pity the tender cries of the sheep. It is a splendid assertion of the power of meekness, as the gold of the lion's "bright mane" becomes an aureole.

But pastoral celebration does not contain all that Blake wishes to say. "The School Boy," while it seems spoken in trust of parents' understanding, is a lament against restriction. It is one of the poems that await the coming into existence of the *Songs of Experience,* where, five years later, it was placed. Other poems are less clear cases. "Holy Thursday" presents the Ascension Day "anniversary" of the charity school children. The "grey-headed beadles" who lead the children into St. Paul's are mentioned first, and they may seem like threatening figures with their "wands white as snow." But the children flow like a river, they are like flowers, they have a "radiance all their own," and they raise their choral voice "like a mighty wind" or "like harmonious thunderings the seats of Heavens among." And, as is usual in these poems, the closing lines have gained meaning from the whole poem. Now the formidable beadles take their place below the angelic children:

> Beneath them sat the aged men, wise guardians of the poor;
> Then cherish pity, lest you drive an angel from your door.

The last line seems pat and inadequate to those who are on the watch for irony; yet it converts the aged men to the counterparts of Abraham and Lot, who entertained angels at their door and were shown favor.

In "The Little Black Boy" the pain of being born with a different face is genuine and acute. Blake enters imaginatively into the condition of the boy and his mother. She supplies a consoling vision that makes the suffering temporary and even a source of pride. By showing her boy that the body is a "cloud" that absorbs the beams of God's love and vanishes after a short term of trial, she turns upside down the standards of the world around him. This can save his sense of worth. His body is better adapted than the white boy's to bearing God's love (God is here conceived much as in Milton, where He dwells in "unapproached light" which the angels can bear to behold only when they veil their eyes with their wings). And all bodies are the instruments by which we are trained to live in the spirit.

The poem ends with a reversal like the one that sets the ominous beadles below the angelic children of "Holy Thursday." The little black boy sees himself with the English child in heaven:

> I'll shade him from the heat, till he can bear
> To lean in joy upon our father's knee;
> And then I'll stand and stroke his silver hair,
> And be like him, and he will then love me.

One can see pathos, surely, in the fundamental desire to "be like him" —the lack of any image of oneself that can give repose or self-respect. Yet there is also a strain of mature understanding or even pity in the recognition that the white boy can bear less love and can give less love —that he needs to wait for the black boy to be like him before he can recognize their oneness in a common father. We may deplore the comparative quietism of this, but we must recognize a faith that permits the boy to live with the inevitable without surrendering to it.

"The Chimney Sweeper" descends farther into suffering, and the plight of the sweeps is as grim as can be conceived. What the poem is saying, nevertheless, is that the naïve faith we see in Tom's dream is the means of survival. In a "Song by an Old Shepherd" Blake had written:

> Blow, boisterous wind, stern winter frown,
> Innocence is a winter's gown;
> So clad, we'll abide life's pelting storm
> That makes our limbs quake, if our hearts be warm.

(64)

The chimney sweep, Tom, dreams that thousands of sweepers are "lock'd up in coffins of black," when

> . . . by came an Angel who had a bright key,
> And he open'd the coffins & set them all free;
> Then down a green plain leaping, laughing, they run,
> And wash in a river, and shine in the Sun.

The Angel is like those in "Night" who receive the wolves' victims, "New worlds to inherit." Here the new world is the miserable child's vision of a heaven—green plains, a river to wash in, sunlight, play, a father. The old world is still there when Tom awakens, but Tom and his companions have a "winter's gown":

> Tho' the morning was cold, Tom was happy & warm;
> So if all do their duty they need not fear harm.

The last line stings with irony as we think of the duties left unperformed by the boys' elders, and it has pathos if we take it to imply that Tom expects virtue to be rewarded in the world. But it is also a daring assertion of naïve faith, the faith that will inevitably be rewarded in its own terms, with an assurance of spirit that can transcend its worldly conditions. This naïve faith has both the precariousness and the strength of a pastoral vision: it seems too fragile to survive suffering, yet it somehow does survive, more vivid and intense than the world it transcends.

I have spoken of these assertions as metaphors for adult existence, and we can see their counterpart in Blake's letters:

> . . . now I have lamented over the dead horse let me laugh & be merry with my friends till Christmas, for as Man liveth not by bread alone, I shall live altho' I should want bread—nothing is necessary to me but to do my Duty & to rejoice in the exceeding joy that is always poured on my Spirit.

(To William Hayley, 7 October 1803)

. . . as none on Earth can give me Mental Distress, & I know that all
Distress inflicted by Heaven is a Mercy, a Fig for all corporeal! Such
Distress is My mock & scorn.

(To Thos. Butts, 11 September 1801)

In "The Little Girl Lost" and "The Little Girl Found" we come to
the borderland between Innocence and Experience. Blake moved these
poems from one group to the other, and this convertibility helps us
understand the relationship of "contrary states." In the two border
poems, the seeming forces of evil prove to be as gentle and fostering as
parents—perhaps through the influence of the sleeping maid, whose
innocence creates a precinct of "hallow'd ground." The lion's "ruby
tears" flow with pity for her unprotectedness: her weakness and her
trust disarm the beasts of prey. In the second poem the lion reveals an
angel within, and his cave becomes a palace; the parents who brave
the wilds for the sake of their lost child are rewarded with a new freedom and security:

> To this day they dwell
> In a lonely dell;
> Nor fear the wolvish howl
> Nor the lions' growl.

They live in a world where evil has no power, however it may seem
to threaten others.

If we stress the faith that is strong enough to transcend the power
of the world, these poems clearly fall into the pattern of Innocence. If,
on the other hand, we stress the adversity to be overcome and the
courage with which it is faced, they move toward Experience, although
they remain the most triumphant of the *Song of Experience*. Seven-
year-old Lyca wanders into the "desart wild" and is lost. Significantly,
she is concerned not for herself but for her parents' grief. She confi-
dently summons the moon to guard her and goes to sleep. The beasts of
the wild play around her body, licking her and weeping with pity, until
at last they accept her as one of themselves, loose her dress, and carry
her to their caves. In "The Little Girl Found" we see that Lyca's
parents do indeed grieve and search for her (as parents in Innocence
do). After seven days of anxiety and distress, the mother can go no
farther and is carried in her husband's arms. They too encounter a
lion, which seems to stalk them. But suddenly he licks their hands and
becomes a "Spirit arm'd in gold" (like the lion in "Night"). He leads
them to his palace where Lyca lies sleeping among "tygers wild."

The strength of Experience comes of its ability to sustain or recover the faith of Innocence. The state of Experience is one of suffering, but we have already seen much of that in Innocence. More significant is the attitude taken toward suffering: those who are frustrated and corrupted by it, surrender; those who seek their freedom and keep their vision alive, rebel. In some poems only the condition of suffering is given: these contribute to that composite image, the contrary of the pastoral vision of Innocence, of a world to be met with either despair or defiance. In "A Little Girl Lost," Ona is terrified by the father whose "loving look" is the face of the punitive moralist, professing (sincerely enough) anxiety for his straying child, but scarcely concealing the self-pity of the rigid lawmaker. In "A Little Boy Lost" the Cordelia-like protestations of the boy lead to his torture and murder by the priests.

In other poems the surrender is clear. In "The Angel" and "My Pretty Rose Tree," life is rejected for the sake of chastity or possessiveness; and the result is armed fear or resentment. The "Nurse's Song" is the expression of anxiety and envy; the repressive nurse is projecting doubts of her own self into the lives of the children. In "The Sick Rose," the secrecy of love becomes disease. The "crimson joy" suggests the rose's complicity both in passion and in secrecy; disguise destroys from within. We see this more clearly in "The Lilly," where the modest rose and the humble sheep protect themselves with a thorn and a threatening horn; whereas the lily's open delight in love makes her whiteness incapable of stain, as is the case with Oothoon later in the *Visions of the Daughters of Albion*.

The central distinction between honest wrath and stifled or corrupted energy is given in the opening poems of the *Songs of Experience*. "Introduction" announces the visionary Bard

> Whose ears have heard
> The Holy Word
> That walk'd among the ancient trees,
>
> Calling the lapsed Soul,
> And weeping in the evening dew;
> That might controll
> The starry pole,
> And fallen, fallen light renew!

(3–10)

"Controll" here still carries the sense of "contradict" or "disprove." The Holy Word is the Poetic Genius within man summoning the dawn of revived life. "Earth's Answer" comes out of "grey despair"; Earth's locks are as gray as those of the virgin who resists love in "The Angel." She can see only the God she has created for herself:

> Prison'd on wat'ry shore,
> Starry Jealousy does keep my den:
> Cold and hoar,
> Weeping o'er,
> I hear the Father of the ancient men.
>
> Selfish father of men!
> Cruel, jealous, selfish fear!
> Can delight,
> Chain'd in night,
> The virgins of youth and morning bear?

(6–15)

Are we to take Earth's words as a just condemnation of the Holy Word, or is Earth's despair the counterpart of the resentment of Adam and Eve in their fallen state, before they recover the power to love and recognize that their Judge is also their Redeemer? The latter seems the more plausible.

"The Tyger" is the best known of Blake's songs and the most frequently and elaborately interpreted. The phrase "fearful symmetry" —whatever its possible symbolic suggestions—is clearly the initial puzzle: the "symmetry" implies an ordering hand or intelligence, the "fearful" throws doubt on the benevolence of the Creator. The "forests of the night" are the darkness out of which the tiger looms, brilliant in contrast; they also embody the doubt or confusion that surrounds the origins of the tiger. In the case of "The Lamb," the Creator "calls himself a Lamb. / He is meek, & he is mild; / He became a little child." In "The Tyger" the Creator again is like what he creates, and the form that must be supplied him now is the Promethean smith working violently at his forge. The last alteration we have of this much altered poem insists upon the likeness of Creator and created: "What dread hand Form'd thy dread feet?" The tiger is an image of the Creator; its "deadly terrors" must be His.

The most puzzling stanza of the poem is the next-to-last:

> When the stars threw down their spears,
> And water'd heaven with their tears,
> Did he smile his work to see?
> Did he who made the Lamb make thee?

The first two lines are the crux of the poem. Are the tears the rage of the defeated, or the tears of mercy as in a later Notebook poem, "Morning"?

> To find the Western path
> Right thro' the Gates of Wrath
> I urge my way;
> Sweet Mercy leads me on:
> With soft repentant moan
> I see the break of day.
>
> The war of swords & spears
> Melted by dewy tears
> Exhales on high;
> The sun is freed from fears
> And with soft grateful tears
> Ascends the sky.

(421)

Here we come through wrath to mercy, through night to dawn. This progression appears again in *Jerusalem,* where Los, the imaginative power, considers his task as visionary poet. Los is seeking to make error visible so that it may be thrown off, and his satiric task requires him to adopt the "forms of cruelty."

> I took the sighs & tears & bitter groans,
> I lifted them into my Furnaces to form the spiritual sword
> That lays open the hidden heart. I drew forth the pang
> Of sorrow red hot: I work'd it on my resolute anvil . . .
> I labour day and night. I behold the soft affections
> Condense beneath my hammer into forms of cruelty,
> But still I labour in hope; tho' still my tears flow down:
> That he who will not defend Truth may be compell'd to defend
> A Lie: that he may be snared and caught and snared and taken:
> That Enthusiasm and Life may not cease . . . .

(9:17–20, 26–31)

The "spiritual sword / That lays open the hidden heart" is a counterpart of the tiger we see in the *Songs of Experience.* The wrath serves the ultimate end of redemption and becomes one with mercy. If the God of apparent wrath is also the God of forgiveness, the tiger's form is only superficially "fearful." In the words of Pope:

> Nor God alone in the still calm we find,
> He mounts the storm, and walks upon the wind.

(*Essay on Man,* II, 109–10)

"The Tyger" dramatizes the terrors of the shocked doubter, but it moves with assurance—in the stanza I have quoted—to an assertion of faith (faith in the oneness of God, in the goodness of wrath, in the holiness of prophetic rage). When the last stanza repeats the first, but for the alteration of "could" to "dare" the question has been answered. The inconceivable of the first stanza has become the majestic certainty of the last: the daring of the Creator—whether God or man—is the cleansing wrath of the tiger.

The honest wrath that is celebrated in "The Tyger" is the open and healthy response to suffering. In contrast, as we have seen, is the tortured brooding of the bound infant who sulks upon his mother's breast, or the viciousness that comes of "unacted desires" in "A Poison Tree." In "London" this pattern of externally imposed suppression (the swaddling bands of the infant, the binding with briars by priests in black gowns) or internal self-imposed repression (the armed fears of the virgin, the secret love of the rose) becomes a general condition whose meaning is evident only to the visionary poet. He alone sees and hears what others take for granted.

> In every cry of every Man,
> In every Infant's cry of fear,
> In every voice, in every ban,
> The mind-forg'd manacles I hear.

The power to penetrate the conventional sounds—whether street cries, oaths, infants' wails—makes the self-imposed tortures of man not simply audible but visible. The cry of the soot-covered chimney sweeper appalls—blackens as much as shocks, convicts as much as arouses—"every black'ning Church" (blackening with the guilt of its indifference far more than with soot). So too the "hapless Soldier's sigh" brands the palace he has been suffering to defend with the guilt of causing his pain; and—sound made visible—"Runs in blood down Palace walls."

> But most thro' midnight streets I hear
> How the youthful Harlot's curse
> Blasts the new born Infant's tear,
> And blights with plagues the Marriage hearse.

The visible stain has become a virulent infection, and its power is caught in the terrible poetic condensation that sees the marriage coach as already a hearse. The existence of the youthful harlot (another conventional street sound, as she curses in the night) is more than a source of physical infection; it is a symptom of the moral disease evident only to the visionary poet. Except for his, there is no open rebellion in this London, no deeply felt outrage. Each cry or sigh or curse arises from a single individual's grief. Only the poet hears what is *in* each cry or sees *how* it looks and acts—in short, what it means. The gap between the suffering and the awareness is part of the terror of the London Blake presents; it is made all the sharper if we contrast the isolated suffering of these cries with the echoing responsiveness on the village green of Innocence.

Only when we grant Innocence its proper value does the full dialectical force of the two contrary states become clear. We can see the potential suffering that surrounds the world of Innocence and the potential triumph that Experience permits. Blake is less concerned with exposing injustice than with finding a vital response to it. The evil he presents is in each case the denial of life, whether imposed from without by society or made within by the individual. The good he espouses is the life-giving vision, whether serenely enjoyed or indignantly defended. Clearly serene transcendence of evil is seldom possible although, as we have seen, Blake rejoices in such moments. And Innocence, like Experience, has its false aspect as well as its true.

In the manuscript of *The Four Zoas* Blake made this note: "Unorganiz'd Innocence: An Impossibility. Innocence dwells with Wisdom, but never with Ignorance" (380). Wisdom need not imply self-consciousness or acquaintance with evil, any more than it does for Adam in Milton's Paradise. But in the years that intervened between the first engraving of the *Songs of Innocence* in 1789 and their yoking to the new *Songs of Experience* in 1793, Blake explored the varieties of false Innocence, which is a denial of life rather than a confident assertion of its goodness.

Infinite London

by David V. Erdman

O Earth O Earth return!
Arise from out the dewy grass;
Night is worn,
And the morn
Rises from the slumberous mass.

—Introduction, *Songs of Experience*

The Bard who recites the *Songs of Experience*, written in 1792–
1793,[1] is capable of seeing "Present, Past, & Future"; yet he must chide
Earth's "lapsed Soul" for the tardiness of spring thaw; and *Earth's
Answer* is really, like the questions of Oothoon, an unanswered appeal
for help to "Break this heavy chain, That does freeze my bones
around." "Cruel jealous selfish fear" (like Fayette's) chains Earth with
winter frost; no one can plow or sow; the buds and blossoms are re-
tarded—for Love is held in bondage.

The complaint is essentially that the revolutionary spring torrent,
which in 1792 seemed to be "spreading and swelling . . . to fertilize
a world, and renovate old earth" (as Holcroft exclaimed in a prologue
in March)[2] is still in England dammed and frozen by cold abstrac-

---

From Chapter 13, "Infinite London," in David V. Erdman, Blake: Prophet Against
Empire, *revised edition to be published in 1969 by Princeton University Press and
Doubleday Anchor Books. Copyright © 1954 by Princeton University Press. Re-
printed by permission of the publisher.*

[1] All eighteen of the *Songs of Experience* in *N.*, including the *Motto to Songs of
Innocence & of Experience*, precede the draft of *Fayette*. In the Prospectus of Oct.
10, 1793, *Songs of Innocence* and *Songs of Experience* are advertised separately. But
all extant copies of the latter have a publication date of 1794 and appear not to
have been issued except in combination with, or to complement earlier copies of,
Songs of Innocence.

The Bard's plea, *Introduction*, is not in *N.* [*Notebooks*], but it must have been
drafted before *Earth's Answer*, which is.

[2] Prologue to *Road to Ruin* as read March 1, 1792; quoted in *London Chronicle*
of March 3.

tions and proclamations of "Thou shalt not." The Bard is determined
that the spring *shall* come; that Earth from sleep

> Shall arise and seek
> For her maker meek:
> And the desart wild
> Become a garden mild.

And he trusts that his own art has ritual force: "Grave the sentence
deep." Yet the poem bearing these declarations was at first a Song of
Innocence, moved now into the contrary group to say what it was
perhaps no longer easy to write.[3]

Now, in his notebook, he wrote a song lamenting that a "heavy
rain" of cruelty, disguised in the specious abstractions of "Mercy &
Pity & Peace," has descended on "the new reapd grain"; the farmers
are "ruind & harvest . . . ended."[4] In an earlier and crueler mood
Blake had written and even etched on copper a bitter characterization
of the kind of *Divine Image* which Cruelty, Jealousy, Terror, and
Secrecy were giving to the nation:

> The Human Dress. is forged Iron
> The Human Form. a fiery Forge.
> The Human Face. a Furnace seal'd
> The Human Heart. its hungry Gorge.[5]

But he kept the copper without printing from it, choosing instead to
stay closer to the ruined grain and farmers. With a more intellectual
irony he constructed from the psychological and moral gains of "mutual fear" and "selfish loves" a song of *The Human Abstract* to sing
against the *Divine Image* of Innocence.

Blake retained his sense of balance by engraving together his *Songs
of Innocence and of Experience* as "contrary states of the human soul,"
and his sense of perspective by treating winter as a season and life as
an arc of Eternity. "Without contraries is no progression," he still
asserts. Yet the peculiar anguish of these songs (and several notebook
pieces of the same vintage) derives from the fact that the historical

---

[3] *The Little Girl Lost: P.&P.* [*The Poetry and Prose of William Blake,* ed. David
V. Erdman, commentary by Harold Bloom (Garden City, N.Y.: 1965), hereafter re-
ferred to as *P.&P.*—Ed.] 20–21. This and *The Voice of the Ancient Bard,* transferred
from *Songs of Innocence,* carry over into *Songs of Experience* a bardic optimism that
is not explicit in the *Introduction.* But *The Schoolboy* (see above) must have been
similarly transferred because it was too gloomy for *Innocence.*

[4] *N.* 114: *P.&P.* 468, 771, "I heard an Angel singing."

[5] *A Divine Image: P.&P.* 32. The script indicates a date of ca. 1791.

contraries of peace and war, freedom and chains, have come to England in the wrong order. For it is only contrary states of the soul, not of society, that exist in Eternity, and Blake is still firm in the belief that the blighting Code of War & Lust is historically negatable. The earth will "in futurity" be a garden; readers "of the future age" will be shocked to learn "that in a former time, Love! sweet Love! was thought a crime." [6]

Relatively little of the considerable and increasing store of commentary on the *Songs of Experience* deals with their historical matrix; yet it would be pedantic here to spell out the application to these songs of much in the preceeding chapters or to go beyond calling attention to the particular setting of some of their major themes. Though immeasurably closer than the prophecies to Blake's ideal of an art that rises above its age "perfect and eternal," these great lyrics soar up from a particular moment of history. The fused brilliance of *London* and *The Tyger*, the sharp, poignant symbolism of *The Garden of Love*, *Infant Sorrow*, and many another "indignant page" were forged in the heat of the Year One of Equality (September 1792 to 1793) and tempered in the "grey-brow'd snows" of Antijacobin alarms and proclamations.

The fearful symmetry of the period in its cosmic implications produced Blake's boldest Oothoonian question, *The Tyger*, touched upon in an earlier chapter. The recurrent negative theme in the Songs is the mental bondage of Antijacobinism, manifest not in the windy caves of Parliament or the archetypal howlings of Albion's Guardians but in the lives of children and youth forced into harlotry and soldiery and apprentice slavery by the bone-bending, mind-chaining oppressions of priest and king. In *Europe* and *America* Blake sketches a panoramic view of the youth of England and their parents walking heavy and mustering for slaughter while their minds are choked by volumes of fog which pour down from "Infinite London's awful spires" and from the palace walls and "cast a dreadful cold Even on rational things beneath." In *Songs of Experience* he takes us into the dismal streets and into schoolroom and chapel to see the effects of Empire on the human "flowers of London town." He describes, in *The Human Abstract*, the growth of the evil tree which is gallows, cross, and the abstract Mystery that hides the facts of war. The roots of this oak or upas tree of perverted Druidism are watered by the selfish tears of Mercy, Pity, and Peace:

[6] *A Little Girl Lost: P.&P.* 29.

> Pity would be no more,
> If we did not make somebody Poor;
> And Mercy no more could be,
> If all were as happy as we;
>
> And mutual fear brings peace;
> Till the selfish loves increase.

This tree grows "in the Human brain," planted there by priest and king, who use the virtuousness of pity as an excuse for poverty and who define peace as an armistice of fear—and thus "promote war." [7]

It is instructive to note that ideas like these were widely propagated in the latter part of 1792 by an Association for Preserving Liberty and Property against Republicans and Levellers—expressly to persuade "the minds of ignorant men" that all causes of discontent were either inescapable or wholly imaginary, and to prepare these minds for the eventuality of England's being "dragged into a French war." [8]

These pamphleteers were in favor of the mutual fear and "military policy" that temporarily bring peace and ultimately bring war.[9] And they bluntly defended the inequality that supports pity and mercy. Both the Bible and "experience," they said, tell us that "society cannot exist without a class of poor." Consequently it is our duty to teach the poor that their sufferings are necessary and natural and not to be remedied by laws or constitutional changes—that it is in fact the object of our maligned and "most excellent Government to alleviate poverty" by "poor laws, work-houses and hospitals," [10] Blake's suspicion that "Churches; Hospitals; Castles; Palaces" are the "nets & gins & traps" of the "Code of War" [11] is confirmed by these anti-levellers: "Every step . . . which can be taken to bind man to man, order to order, the lower to the higher, the poor to the rich, is now a more peculiar

[7] *The Human Abstract* and draft called *The Human Image* (N. 107) in which the "mystery" is discussed that "The priest promotes war & the soldier peace." Cf. Marg. to Watson, iv: *P.&P.* 601. For a discussion of the relations of these poems and of the internal evidence for an early date for *A Divine Image* (confirmed now by script) see Robert F. Gleckner, *PMLA*, LXXVI, 1961, 373–379.

[8] I quote from *Politics . . . Reflections on the Present State of Affairs*, by a Lover of His Country, Edinburgh, 1792. For the Association, see *London Chronicle*, Nov. 27–29, 1792.

[9] *Politics*. On the one hand, peace is "an object of desire" most effectually approached, we are told, by "a military policy" and increased armaments; on the other hand, if our "great empire is insulted by the impudent memorials of a set of plunderers" (the rulers of France) war will be "necessary and unavoidable."

[10] William Vincent, *A Discourse to the People*, London, 1792.

[11] *Song of Los: P.&P.* 66.

duty; and if there are any means to prevent the spreading of dangerous and delusive principles, they must be sought for in education.
[Hence the need for] Foundation Schools, Hospitals, Parish Schools,
and Sunday Schools." [12]

Blake's counterargument is that if there were not "so many children
poor" there would be no need for institutions and moral code—and
no ignorant men for sale to the fat fed hireling. Poverty appalls the
mind, making youth sufficiently docile to be led "to slaughter houses"
and beauty sufficiently desperate to be "bought & sold . . . for a bit
of bread" (*N.* 107). There can be no vital bond of man to man in such
"a land of Poverty!" Starvation demonstrates the absurdity of the
anti-vice campaign, for the church remains spiritually and physically
a cold barn, to which *The Little Vagabond* rightly prefers the warm
tavern.[13] The harlot's curse will weave Old England's winding sheet,
and ultimately the raging desire for bread will undermine the whole
misery-built London of spire and palace.

Boston's Angel asked, "What crawling villain preaches abstinence
& wraps himself In fat of lambs?" The chimney sweep, a "little black
thing among the snow," answers that it is

> God & his Priest & King,
> Who wrap themselves up in our misery [*deleted reading*]
> And because I am happy & dance & sing
> They think they have done me no injury.

> (*N.* 103)

King, priest, god, and parents do not reckon the revolutionary potential in the multitude they are stripping naked. Yet even the sheep puts
forth "a threatning horn" against the tithing priest (*N.* 109). As for the
chimney sweeper, his father and mother have turned a happy boy into
a symbol of death. Once a year he still does dance and sing—on May

---

[12] Vincent.
[13] A curious "mark of weakness" appears in Blake's own publication. In etching the
Vagabond, Blake bowdlerized the fourth line, changing "makes all go to hell" to "will
never do well," thereby introducing a bad rime and an ambiguity rather than defy
the moral code of the Vice Society. The first notebook draft (*N.* 105) reads:

> Dear Mother Dear Mother the church is cold
> But the alehouse is healthy & pleasant & warm
> Besides I can tell where I am usd well,
> Such usage in heaven makes all go to hell.

Even as published, the "audacity" and "mood of this wild poem" disturbed Coleridge
in 1818. *Collected Letters,* ed. E. L. Griggs, IV, 834–838.

Day, when London streets are given to the sweeps and milkmaids to perform for alms in grotesque symmetry.[14] *The Chimney Sweeper* is saying to the London citizen: you salve your conscience by handing out a few farthings on May Day, but if you really listened to this bitter cry among the snow you and your icy church would be appalled.

When we turn now to *London*, Blake's "mightiest brief poem,"[15] our minds ringing with Blakean themes, we come upon infinite curses in a little room, a world at war in a grain of London soot. On the illuminated page a child is leading a bent old man along the cobblestones and a little vagabond . . . is warming his hands at a fire in the open street. But it is Blake who speaks.

London

> I wander thro' each charter'd street,
> Near where the charter'd Thames does flow.
> And mark in every face I meet
> Marks of weakness, marks of woe.
>
> In every cry of every Man,
> In every Infants cry of fear,
> In every voice: in every ban,
> The mind-forg'd manacles I hear.
>
> How the Chimney-sweepers cry
> Every blackning Church appalls,
> And the hapless Soldiers sigh,
> Runs in blood down Palace walls[16]
>
> But most thro' midnight streets I hear
> How the youthful Harlots curse
> Blasts the new-born Infants tear
> And blights with plagues the Marriage hearse

In his first draft Blake wrote "dirty street" and "dirty Thames" as plain statement of fact, reversing the sarcastic "golden London" and "silver Thames" of his early parody of Thomson's *Rule Britannia*. And the

[14] I refer to an ancient May Day custom, illustrated by Blake in 1784 in an engraving for the *Wit's Magazine,* after Collings. The picture, *May Day,* is still used in works illustrating social customs. Milkmaids danced with pitcher-laden trays on their heads; the sweeps, with wigs to cover their grimy heads, banged their brushes and scrapers in rhythm; and a fiddler or two supplied a tune. Reproduced in *Johnson's England,* ed. A. S. Turberville, I, 174.

[15] Oliver Elton's phrase, I forget where.

[16] The poem originally ended here. See *N.* 109: *P.&P.* 718–719.

harlot's curse sounded in every "dismal" street. The change to "charter'd" (with an intermediate "cheating")[17] mocks Thomson's boast
that "the charter of the land" keeps Britons free, and it suggests agreement with (perhaps was even suggested by) Paine's condemnation of
"charters and corporations" in the Second Part of *The Rights of Man,*
where Paine argues that all charters are purely negative in effect and
that city charters, by annulling the rights of the majority, cheat the inhabitants and destroy the town's prosperity—even London being "capable of bearing up against the political evils of a corporation" only
from its advantageous situation on the Thames.[18] Paine's work was
circulated by shopkeepers chafing under corporation rule and weary,
like Blake, of the "cheating waves of charterd streams" of monopo-
lized commerce (*N.* 113).

In the notebook fragment just quoted Blake speaks of shrinking "at
the little blasts of fear That the hireling blows into my ear," thus indi-
cating that when he writes of the "mind-forg'd manacles" in every cry
of fear and every ban he is not saying simply that people are voluntarily
forging manacles in their own minds. Hireling informers or mercenaries promote the fear; Pitt's proclamations are the bans, linked with
an order to dragoons "to assemble on Hounslow Heath" and "be within
one hour's march of the metropolis." [19] A rejected reading, "german
forged links," points to several manacles forged ostensibly in the mind
of Hanoverian George: the Prussian maneuvres on the heath, the
British alliance with Prussia and Austria against France, and the land-
ing of Hessian and Hanoverian mercenaries in England allegedly en
route to battlefronts in France.

Blake may have written *London* before this last development, but
before he completed his publication there was a flurry of alarm among
freeborn Englishmen at the presence of German hirelings. "Will you
wait till BARRACKS are erected in every village," exclaimed a London
Corresponding Society speaker in January 1794, "and till subsidized
Hessians and Hanoverians are upon us?" [20] In Parliament Lord Stan-
hope expressed the hope that honest Britons would meet this Prussian

---

[17] The "cheating" variant is in *N.* 113; see *P.&P.* 464, 772.
[18] Paine, I, 407. On chartered boroughs see Cowper, *The Task*, iv. 671. J. T. Boulton, *The Language of Politics in the Age of Wilkes and Burke*, 1963, p. 193, cites a
likely source in a 1791 pamphlet reply to Burke: "What is Great Britain . . . but a
charter'd isle, and every city, town borough, and cinque port, have their charters
also." John Butler, *Brief Reflections upon the Liberty of the British Subject.*
[19] *Gazette*, Dec. 1, 1792.
[20] Address at Globe Tavern, Jan. 20, 1794 (pamphlet).

invasion "by OPPOSING FORCE BY FORCE." And the editor of *Politics for the People*, reporting that one Hessian had stabbed an Englishman in a street quarrel, cried that all were brought "to cut the throats of Englishmen." He urged citizens to arm and to fraternize with their fellow countrymen, the British common soldiers.[21]

The latter are Blake's "hapless Soldiers" whose "sigh Runs in blood down Palace walls"—and whose frequently exhibited inclination in 1792–1793 to turn from grumbling to mutiny[22] is not taken into account by those who interpret the blood as the soldier's own and who overlook the potentially forceful meaning of "sigh" in eighteenth century diction.[23] In the structure of the poem the soldier's utterance that puts blood on palace walls is parallel to the harlot's curse that blasts and blights. And Blake would have known that curses were often chalked or painted on the royal walls. In October 1792 Lady Malmesbury's Louisa saw "written upon the Privy Garden-wall, 'No coach-tax; d—— Pitt! d——n the Duke of Richmond! *no King!*' "[24]

A number of cognate passages in which Blake mentions blood on palace walls indicate that the blood is an apocalyptic omen of mutiny and civil war involving regicide. In *The French Revolution* people and soldiers fraternize, and when their "murmur" (sigh) reaches the palace, blood runs down the ancient pillars. In *The Four Zoas*, Night I, similar "wailing" affects the people; "But most the polish'd Palaces, dark, silent, bow with dread." "But most" is a phrase straight from *London*.

[21] Eaton, *Politics for the People*, II, no. 7, March 15, 1794.

[22] The Royal Proclamation cited efforts to "delude the judgment of the lower classes" and "debauch the soldiery." Wilberforce feared that "the soldiers are everywhere tampered with." Gilbert Elliot, in November 1792, expressed a common belief that armies and navies would prove "but brittle weapons" against the spreading French ideas. Elliot, II, 74. Through the winter and spring there were sporadic attacks of the populace on press gangs and recruiting houses. Mutiny and rumors of mutiny were reported in the *General Evening Post*, Apr. 20, July 20, Aug. 3, 7, 31, Oct. 28, 30, 1793. In Ireland the mutiny of embodied regiments broached into a small civil war. See also Werkmeister, items indexed under "Insurrection, phantom," and "Ireland."

[23] Damon, p. 283, reads it as the battlefield "death-sigh" which morally "is a stain upon the State." Joseph H. Wicksteed, *Blake's Innocence & Experience*, N.Y., 1928, p. 253, has it that the soldier who promotes peace is quelling the "tumult and war" of a "radically unstable" society. But Blake was not one to look upon riot-quelling as a securing of freedom and peace! Alfred Kazin, *The Portable Blake*, p. 15, with a suggestion "that the Soldier's desperation runs, like his own blood, in accusation down the walls of the ruling Palace," comes closer to the spirit of indignation which Blake reflects.

[24] Elliot, II, 71. Verbally Blake's epithet may be traced back, I suppose, to "hapless Warren!", Barlow's phrase for the patriot general dying at Bunker Hill (changed to "glorious Warren" in 1793).

And in Night IX the people's sighs and cries of fear mount to "furious" rage, apocalyptic blood "pours down incessant," and "Kings in their palaces lie drown'd" in it, torn "limb from limb." [25] In the same passage the marks of weakness and woe of *London* are spelled out as "all the marks . . . of the slave's scourge & tyrant's crown." In *London* Blake is talking about what he hears in the streets, not about the moral stain of the battlefield sigh of expiring soldiers.

In Blake's notebook the lines called *An Ancient Proverb* recapitulate the *London* theme in the form of a Bastille Day recipe for freeing Old England from further plagues of tyranny:

> Remove away that blackning church
> Remove away that marriage hearse
> Remove away that ——— of blood
> Youll quite remove the ancient curse

Where he might have written "palace" he cautiously writes a dash.[26] Yet despite the occasional shrinking of Blake as citizen, Blake as prophet, from *The French Revolution* to *The Song of Los,* from 1791 to 1795, cleaved to the vision of an imminent spring thaw when the happy earth would "sing in its course" as the fire of Voltaire and Rousseau melted the Alpine or Atlantic snows. In England, nevertheless, the stubborn frost persisted and the wintry dark; and England's crisis and Earth's crisis were threatening to become permanent.

[25] *F.R.* [*The French Revolution*] 241–246: *P.&P.* 293; *F.Z.* [*The Four Zoas*] i:14:15–18: *P.&P.* 304; ix.119:7–8: *P.&P.* 373; ix.119:7–8: *P.&P.* 373; ix.123:5–10: *P.&P.* 377.
[26] *N.* 107: *P.&P.* 466, 773. Blake's dash, an unusual mark for him, replaces an earlier "man" which replaced a still earlier "place." The "man of blood" would be the King, but Blake wanted the *place,* i.e. the Palace and so settled for a dash.

Blake's Introduction to Experience

by Northrop Frye

Students of literature often think of Blake as the author of a number of lyrical poems of the most transparent simplicity, and of a number of "prophecies" of the most impenetrable complexity. The prophecies are the subject of some bulky commentaries, including one by the present writer, which seem to suggest that they are a special interest, and may not even be primarily a literary one. The ordinary reader is thus apt to make a sharp distinction between the lyrical poems and the prophecies, often with a hazy and quite erroneous notion in his mind that the prophecies are later than the lyrics, and represent some kind of mental breakdown.

Actually Blake, however versatile, is rigorously consistent in both his theory and practice as an artist. The *Poetical Sketches,* written mostly in his teens, contain early lyrics and early prophecies in about equal proportions. While he was working on the *Songs of Innocence and Experience,* he was also working on their prophetic counterparts. While he was working at Felpham on his three most elaborate prophecies, he was also writing the poems in the Pickering MS, which include such pellucid lyrics as "Mary," "William Bond," and "The Smile." The extent to which the prophecies themselves are permeated by a warm and simple lyrical feeling may be appreciated by any reader who does not shy at the proper names. Hence the method adopted in some critical studies, including my own *Fearful Symmetry,* of concentrating on the prophecies and neglecting the lyrics on the ground that they can be understood without commentary may have the long-run disadvantage of compromising with a thoroughly mistaken view of Blake.

What I propose to do here is to examine one of Blake's shortest and best-known poems in such a way as to make it an introduction to some of the main principles of Blake's thought. The poem selected is the

"Blake's Introduction to Experience" by Northrop Frye. From Huntington Library Quarterly, *XXI (1957), 57–67. Reprinted by permission.*

"Introduction" to the *Songs of Experience,* which for many reasons is as logical a place as any to begin the study of Blake. I do not claim that the way of reading it set forth here is necessary for all readers, but only that for those interested in further study of Blake it is a valid reading.

> Hear the voice of the Bard!
> Who Present, Past & Future, sees;
> Whose ears have heard
> The Holy Word
> That walk'd among the ancient trees . . .

This stanza tells us a great deal about Blake's view of the place and function of the poet. The second line, repeated many years later in *Jerusalem* ("I see the Past, Present & Future existing all at once Before me"), establishes at once the principle that the imagination unifies time by making the present moment real. In our ordinary experience of time we are aware only of three unrealities: a vanished past, an unborn future, and a present that never quite comes into existence. The center of time is now, yet there never seems to be such a time as now. In the ordinary world we can bind experience together only through the memory, which Blake declares has nothing to do with imagination. There is no contact with any other points of time except those that have apparently disappeared in the past. As Proust says, in such a world our only paradises can be the paradises that we have lost. For Blake, as for Eliot in the "Quartets," there must also be another dimenison of experience, a vertical timeless axis crossing the horizontal flow of time at every moment, providing in that moment a still point of a turning world, a moment neither in nor out of time, a moment that Blake in the prophecies calls the moment in each day that Satan cannot find.

The worst theological error we can make, for Blake, is the "Deist" one of putting God at the beginning of the temporal sequence, as a First Cause. Such a view leads logically to an absolute fatalism, though its devotees are seldom so logical. The only God worth worshipping is a God who, though in his essence timeless, continually enters and redeems time, in other words an incarnate God, a God who is also Man. There is a Trinity in Blake of Father, Son, and Spirit, but Blake takes very seriously the Christian doctrines that the Spirit proceeds from the Son and that no man can know the Father except through the Son, the humanity of God. Attempts to approach the Father directly produce what Blake calls "Nobodaddy," whom we shall meet again in the

next poem "Earth's Answer," and who is the ill-tempered old man in
the sky that results from our efforts to visualize a First Cause. Attempts
to approach the Spirit directly produce the vague millennialism of the
revolutionaries of Blake's time, where human nature as it exists is assumed to be perfectible at some time in the future. What Blake thinks
of this he has expressed in the prose introduction to the third part of
Jerusalem. For Blake there is no God but Jesus, who is also man, and
who exists neither in the past like the historical Jesus, nor in the future
like the Jewish Messiah, but now in a real present, in which the real
past and the real future are contained. The word "eternity" in Blake
means the reality of the present moment, not the indefinite extension
of the temporal sequence.

The modern poet or "Bard" thus finds himself in the tradition of the
Hebrew prophets, who derive their inspiration from Christ as Word
of God, and whose life is a listening for and speaking with that Word.
In the Christian view, as recorded in *Paradise Lost,* it was not the
Father but Jesus who created the unfallen world, placed man in Eden,
and discovered man's fall while "walking in the garden in the cool of
the day" (Gen. iii.8), the passage alluded to in the last line of the stanza.

> Calling the lapsèd Soul,
> And weeping in the evening dew;
> That might controll
> The starry pole,
> And fallen, fallen light renew!

"Calling" refers primarily to Christ, the Holy Word calling Adam
in the garden, and the "lapsed Soul" is presumably Adam, though the
epithet seems curious, as Blake did not believe in a soul, but only in a
spiritual body, as far as individual man is concerned. The word "weeping" also refers primarily to Christ. Neither in the Biblical story nor in
Paradise Lost, where we might expect it, do we get much sense of Christ
as deeply moved by man's fate, except in theory. Blake is making a
much more definite identification than Milton does of Adam's "gracious
Judge, without revile," with the Jesus of the Gospels who wept over
the death of man as typified in Lazarus. Both the calling and the
weeping, of course, are repeated by the Bard; the denunciations of the
prophet and the elegiac vision of the poet of experience derive from
God's concern over fallen man.

In the last three lines the grammatical antecedent of "That" is
"Soul"; hence we seem to be told that man, if he had not fallen, would

have had the powers as well as the destiny of a god. He would not now be subject to an involuntary subordination to a "nature" that alternately freezes and roasts him. On a second look, however, we see that Blake is not saying "might have controlled," but "might controll": the conquest of nature is now within man's powers, and is a conquest to which the poets and prophets are summoning him with the voice of the Word of God. We are very close here to Blake's central doctrine of art, and the reason for his insistence that "Jesus & his Apostles & Disciples were all Artists."

The ordinary world that we see is a mindless chaos held together by automatic order: an impressive ruin, but a "slumberous mass," and not the world man wants to live in. What kind of world man wants to live in is indicated by the kind of world he keeps trying to create: a city and a garden. But his cities and gardens, unlike the New Jerusalem and Eden of the Biblical revelation, are not eternal or infinite, nor are they identical with the body of God. By "Artist" Blake means something more like charitable man or man of visible love. He is the man who lives now in the true world which is man's home, and tries to make that world visible to others. "Let every Christian," urges Blake, "engage himself openly & publicly before all the World in some Mental pursuit for the Building up of Jerusalem."

The second stanza particularly illustrates the fact that what is true of time must be equally true of space. Just as the real form of time is "A vision of the Eternal Now," so the real form of space is "here." Again, in ordinary experience of space, the center of space, which is "here," cannot be located, except vaguely as within a certain area: all experienced space is "there," which is why, when we invent such gods as Nobodaddy, we place them "up there," in the sky and out of sight. But as "eternal" means really present, so "infinite" means really here. Christ is a real presence in space as well as a real present in time, and the poet's imagination has the function of bringing into ordinary experience what is really here and now, the bodily presence of God. Just as there is no God except a God who is also Man, so there is no real man except Jesus, man who is also God. Thus the imagination of the poet, by making concrete and visible a hidden creative power, repeats the Incarnation.

If all times are now in the imagination, all spaces are here. Adam before his fall lived in a Paradisal garden, a garden which is to be one day restored to him, but which since his fall has existed, as Jesus taught, within us, no longer a place but a state of mind. Thus Blake begins

Milton by speaking of his own brain as a part of the Garden of Eden, which his art attempts to realize in the world. In the Bible the Garden of Eden is the imaginative form of what existed in history as the tyrannies of Egypt and Babylon. Similarly the Promised Land, flowing with milk and honey, is the imaginative form of what existed historically as the theocracy of Israel. England, along with America, is also the historical form of what in the imagination is the kingdom of Atlantis, which included both, but now lies under the "Sea of Time and Space" flooding the fallen mind. We begin at this point to see the connection between our present poem and the famous lyric, written much later as a preface to *Milton,* "And did those feet in ancient time." As all imaginative places are the same place, Atlantis, Eden, and the Promised Land are the same place; hence when Christ walked in the Garden of Eden in the cool of the day he was also walking on the spiritual form of England's mountains green, among the "Druid" oaks. We note that Blake speaks in the first line of this poem not of a poet or a prophet but of a "Bard," in his day an almost technical term for a tradition of *British* poets going back to the dawn of history. "All had originally one language, and one religion: this was the religion of Jesus, the Everlasting Gospel."

> O Earth, O Earth, return!
> Arise from out the dewy grass;
> Night is worn,
> And the morn
> Rises from the slumberous mass.

The first words spoken by Jesus through the mouth of his "Bard" are, appropriately enough, quoted from the Hebrew prophets. The first line refers partly to the desperate cry of Jeremiah faced with the invincible stupidity of his king: "O earth, earth, earth, hear the word of the Lord!" (Jer. xxii.29). A century earlier Milton, after twenty years spent in defending the liberty of the English people, helplessly watching them choose "a Captain back for Egypt," could express himself only in the same terms, in a passage at the end of *The Ready and Easy Way* that may have focused Blake's attention on his source:

> Thus much I should perhaps have said, though I were sure I should have spoken only to Trees and Stones; and had none to cry to, but with the Prophet, *O Earth, Earth, Earth!* to tell the very Soil itself, what her perverse inhabitants are deaf to.

There is also an echo in the same line from Isaiah (xxi.11–12):

He calleth to me out of Seir, Watchman, what of the night? Watchman, what of the night? The watchman said, The morning cometh, and also the night: if ye will inquire, inquire ye: return, come.

Both in the Hebrew language and in Blake's, "cometh" could also be rendered by "has come": the light and the darkness are simultaneously with us, one being "here" and the other "there," one trying to shine from within, the other surrounding us. Hence a third Biblical allusion appears dimly but firmly attached to the other two (John i.5): "And the light shineth in darkness; and the darkness comprehended it not." The "fallen light," therefore, is the alternating light and darkness of the world we know; the unfallen light would be the eternal light of the City of God, where there is no longer need for sun or moon, and where we can finally see, as Blake explains in the prophecies, that no creative act of man has, in fact, really disappeared in time.

We notice in this stanza that the "Soul" is now identified, not as Adam, but as "Earth," a being who, as we can see by a glance at the next poem, is female. Thus the "Soul" is a kind of *anima mundi;* she includes not only the individual man and the "Church" but the totality of life, the whole creation that, as Paul says, groaneth and travaileth in pain together until now. She is also Nature red in tooth and claw, the struggle for existence in the animal world, of which man, in his fallen aspect, forms part. The prophet sees in every dawn the image of a resurrection that will lift the world into another state of being altogether. He is always prepared to say "the time is at hand." But every dawn in the world "out there" declines into sunset, as the spinning earth turns away into darkness.

> Turn away no more;
> Why wilt thou turn away?
> The starry floor,
> The wat'ry shore,
> Is giv'n thee till the break of day.

There are two ways of looking at the "fallen" world: as fallen, and as a protection against worse things. Man might conceivably have fallen into total chaos, or nonexistence, or, like Tithonus or Swift's Struldbrugs, he might have been forced to live without the hope of death. This world is pervaded by a force that we call natural law, and natural law, however mindless and automatic, at any rate affords a solid bottom to life: it provides a sense of the predictable and trustworthy on which the imagination may build. The role of natural law (called Bowlahoola in the prophecies) as the basis of imaginative effort is what Blake has in mind when he calls creation "an act of Mercy"; the providential aspect of time, in sweeping everything away into an apparent nonexistence, is brought out in his observation that "Time is the Mercy of Eternity." In the Bible a similar sense of the created world as a protection against chaos, usually symbolized in the Bible by the sea, as a firmament in the midst of the waters, comes out in the verse in Job (xxxviii.11): "Hitherto shalt thou come but no further, and here shall thy proud waves be stayed." It is this verse that Blake has in mind when he speaks of the "wat'ry shore" as given to Earth until the Last Judgment; it is the same guarantee that God gave to Noah in the figure of the rainbow. Similarly the automatic accuracy of the heavenly bodies, of which Earth of course is one, affords a minimum basis for imaginative effort. Newtonian science is quite acceptable to Blake as long as it deals with the automatism of nature as the "floor" and not the ceiling of experience.

In Blake's prophecies there are two perspectives, so to speak, on human life. One is a tragic and ironic vision; the other sees life as part of a redemptive divine comedy. The usual form taken by the tragic vision is that of a cyclical narrative, seen at its fullest and clearest in *The Mental Traveller* and *The Gates of Paradise*. Here there are two main characters, a male figure, the narrator in *The Gates of Paradise* and the "Boy" of *The Mental Traveller,* and a female figure who, in the latter poem, grows younger as the male grows older and vice versa, and who in *The Gates of Paradise* is described as "Wife, Sister, Daughter, to the Tomb."

The "Boy" of *The Mental Traveller* is struggling humanity, called Orc in the prophecies. The female figure is nature, which human culture partially but never completely subdues in a series of historical cycles. The relations between them are roughly those of mother and son, wife and husband, daughter and father. Very roughly, for none of these relations is quite accurate: the mother is an old nurse, the wife merely a temporary possession, and the daughter a changeling. The "Female will," as Blake calls it, has no necessary connection with human women, who are part of humanity, except when a woman wants to make a career of being a "harlot coy," or acting as nature does. The female will is rather the elusive, retreating, mysterious remoteness of the external world.

The "Introduction" to the *Songs of Experience,* despite its deeply serious tone, takes on the whole the redemptive or providential view.

Hence the relation of the two figures is reversed, or rather, as they are not the same figures, the relation of a male and a female figure is used to symbolize the redemption of man instead of his bondage. The two characters correspond to the Bridegroom and Bride of Biblical symbolism. The male character is primarily Christ or the Word of God, which extends to take in the prophets and poets, and is ultimately Christ as the creative power in the whole of humanity. The "Bard" is called Los in the prophecies, the Holy Spirit who proceeds from the Son. The female character Earth embraces everything that Christ is trying to redeem, the forgiven harlot of the Old Testament prophets who keeps turning way from forgiveness. She has no name, as such, in the prophecies, though her different aspects have different names, the most important being Ahania and Enion. She is in general what Blake calls the "emanation," the total form of what man, or rather God in man, is trying to create. This total form, a city, a garden, a home, and a bed of love, or as Blake says "a City, yet a Woman," is Jerusalem. But just as the female will is not necessarily human women, so Earth, the Bride of Christ, includes men, as in the more conventional symbol of the Church.

In her "Answer" Earth rejects with bitterness and some contempt the optimistic tone of the Bard's final words. She does not feel protected; she feels imprisoned, in the situation dramatized in Blake's poem *Visions of the Daughters of Albion*. She recalls Io, guarded by the myriad-eyed Argus, or Andromeda, chained on the seashore and constantly devoured by a possessive jealousy. Earth is not saying, as some critics accuse her of saying, that all would be well if lovers would only learn to copulate in the daytime. She is saying that nearly all of man's creative life remains embryonic, shrouded in darkness, on the level of wish, hope, dream and private fantasy. Man is summoned by the Bard to love the world and let his love shine before men, but his natural tendency, as a child of fallen nature, is the miser's tendency to associate love with some private and secret possession of his own. This "dark secret love," or rather perversion of love, is what Blake means by jealousy.

The "Selfish father of men" who keeps Earth imprisoned is not God the Father, of course, but the false father that man visualizes as soon as he takes his mind off the Incarnation. To make God a Father is to make ourselves children: if we do this in the light of the Gospels, we see the world in the light of the state of innocence. But if we take the point of view of the child of ordinary experience, our God becomes a projection of ordinary childishness, a vision of undeveloped humanity. If we think of God as sulky, capricious, irritable and mindlessly cruel, like Dante's primal love who made hell, or tied in knots of legal quibbles, like Milton's father-god, we may have a very awful divinity, but we have not got a very presentable human being. There is no excuse for keeping such a creature around when we have a clear revelation of God's human nature in the Gospels.

The source of this scarecrow is fallen nature: man makes a gigantic idol out of the dark world, and is so impressed by its stupidity, cruelty, empty spaces, and automatism that he tries to live in accordance with the dreary ideals it suggests. He naturally assumes that his god is jealous of everything he clings to with secret longing and wants it surrendered to him; hence he develops a religion of sacrifice. There are two other reasons for Earth's calling her tormentor the "father of the ancient men." In the first place, he is the ghost of what in the New Testament would be called the first Adam. In the second place, he is the god to whom the "Druids" sacrificed human beings in droves, as an eloquent symbol of their belief, quite true in itself, that their god hated human life. This false father still exists as the shadow thrown by Newtonian science into the stars, or what Blake calls the "Spectre." He is the genius of discouragement, trying to impress us with the reality of the world of experience and the utter unreality of anything better. His chief weapons are moral conformity, sexual shame, and the kind of rationality that always turns out to be anti-intellectual. If we could only get rid of him, "every thing would appear to man as it is, infinite."

In the three characters of these two poems we have the three generating forces, so to speak, of all Blake's symbolism. First is the Bard, representative of the whole class that Blake in *Milton* calls "Reprobate," personified by Los, and including all genuine prophets and artists. They are given this name because their normal social role is that of a persecuted and ridiculed minority. Earth includes the total class of the "Redeemed," or those capable of responding to the Reprobate. In the later prophecies Blake tends to use the masculine and purely human symbol of "Albion" as representing what the prophet tries to redeem. We can see part of the reason for this change in the poems we are studying: the Bard appeals to Earth, but Earth reminds him that man is responsible for his own evils, and that he should talk only to man if he is to do anything to help her.

The father of the ancient men is what in *Milton* is called the "Elect," because the idolatry of fallen nature incarnates itself in all natural societies; that is, the tyrannies of warriors and priests. In *Milton* too the Reprobate and Redeemed are called "Contraries," because the conflict between them is the "Mental fight" in which every man is obligated to engage. The Elect constitutes a "Negation": he is the aspect of the law that the Gospel annihilates, as distinct from the "starry floor," or basis of imaginative order which it fulfills.

Tyger of Wrath

by Morton D. Paley

In peace there's nothing so becomes a man
As modest stillness and humility,
But when the blast of war blows in our ears,
Then imitate the action of the tiger:
Stiffen the sinews, summon up the blood,
Disguise fair nature with hard-favored rage;
Then lend the eye a terrible aspect:
Let it cry through the portage of the head
Like the brass cannon; let the brow o'erwhelm it
As fearfully as doth a galled rock
O'erhang and jutty his confounded base,
Swilled with the wild and wasteful ocean.

Henry V III.i.3–14

How would an ideal contemporary reader of Blake—one of those "Young Men of the New Age" whom he addressed in *Milton*—have regarded "The Tyger"? To such a reader certain aspects of the poem which modern critics have ignored would be obvious. In the rhetoric and imagery of the poem he would recognize an example of the sublime, appropriately Hebrew and terrifying. He would recollect analogues to the wrath of the Tyger in the Old Testament Prophets and in Revelation, and being an ideal reader, he would not need to be reminded that Blake elsewhere views the French Revolution as an eschatological event. He would also know that Blake characteristically thought of divine wrath as an expression of what Jakob Boehme calls the First Principle. His understanding of the poem would thus be affected by his connecting it with the sublime, the Bible, and Boehme.

Reprinted by permission of the Modern Language Association from "Tyger of Wrath" by Morton D. Paley. From Publications of the Modern Language Association, *LXXXI (1966), 540–51. An expanded version of this essay appears in the author's study of Blake,* Energy and the Imagination *(Oxford, 1969).*

We later readers may also discover something about the meaning of "The Tyger" by considering it in relation to these traditions. That such an approach has something new and valuable to offer will be seen if we begin with what has previously been said about the poem.

I

"The Tyger" has always been one of Blake's most admired poems, and it was one of the few to gain even moderate notice in his lifetime. It was one of four Blake lyrics which were copied into Wordsworth's Commonplace Book in 1803 or 1804;[1] it gave Coleridge great pleasure;[2] Lamb thought it "glorious." [3] In 1806 it was printed along with a few of Blake's other lyrics in *A Father's Memoir of His Child* by Benjamin Heath Malkin.[4] It was one of five poems to appear in a German periodical in 1811, along with an article on Blake by Henry Crabb Robinson.[5] Allan Cunningham, in his *Lives of the Most Eminent British Painters, Sculptors, and Architects* (1830), said "The little poem called 'The Tiger' has been admired for the force and vigor of its thoughts by poets of high name." [6] Transcripts must have circulated privately: Damon says that "when the authentic text was published, protests appeared in various magazines, giving the lines 'to which we are accustomed.' " [7]

The poem must have continued to pass from one friend to another after Blake's death (it was, of course, included in J. J. Garth Wilkinson's edition of the *Songs,* published in London in 1839), for Alexander Gilchrist, whose *Life of William Blake* appeared in 1863, wrote: "One

[1] See F. W. Bateson, *Wordsworth, A Re-Interpretation* (London, 1954), p. 133; and *Selected Poems of William Blake* (New York, 1957), p. 116. Professor Bateson has informed me that the handwriting may be Dorothy Wordsworth's.

[2] See letter of 12 February 1818. *Collected Letters,* ed. Earl Leslie Griggs (Oxford, 1959), IV, 836–838.

[3] Letter of 15 May 1824. *The Letters of Charles Lamb & Mary Lamb,* ed. E. V. Lucas (New Haven, 1935), II, 424–427. For Blake's reputation among his contemporaries, see Geoffrey Keynes, "Blake with Lamb and His Circle," *Blake Studies* (London, 1949), pp. 84–104.

[4] London, 1806. The child, who died young, had been a drawing pupil of Blake's. Malkin's comment on "The Tyger" (see below) is slight, but his judicious remarks on some of the other poems entitle him to be considered the first Blake critic.

[5] See Arthur Symons, *William Blake* (London, 1907), pp. 278–279.

[6] Symons, p. 393.

[7] S. Foster Damon, *William Blake: His Philosophy and Symbols* (New York, 1947) [first published 1924], p. 276. [A selection from this book is included among the essays in this volume.—Ed.]

poem in the *Songs of Experience* happens to have been quoted often enough . . . to have made its strange old Hebrew-like grandeur, its Oriental latitude yet force of eloquence, comparatively familiar:— *The Tiger*." [8] The latter part of Gilchrist's statement echoes what Malkin had previously said: "It wears that garb of grandeur, which the idea of the creation communicates to a mind of the higher order. Our bard, having brought the topic he descants on from warmer latitudes than his own, is justified in adopting an imagery, of almost oriental feature and complection." [9] By "Oriental" these writers mean Middle Eastern, Semitic; they recognize, however vaguely, that the poem has an Old Testament model, a fact of some importance to my own view of it.

But none of this so far amounts to interpretation, which begins with the first long critical essay devoted to Blake, Algernon Charles Swinburne's *William Blake,* first published in 1868. Although Swinburne's comments on "The Tyger" are scant, he does begin the long history of critics' attempts to determine its implications. I shall try to indicate what the important representative views have been.

Swinburne reads the poem as a piece of Romantic Satanism. Making use of Blake's Notebook, then in the possession of Dante Gabriel Rossetti, Swinburne prints an earlier version of the second stanza, then paraphrases it and some of the rest of the poem as follows:

> Burnt in distant deeps or skies
> The cruel fire of thine eyes?
> Could heart descend or wings aspire?
> What the hand dare seize the fire?

Could God bring down his heart to the making of a thing so deadly and strong? or could any lesser daemonic force of nature take to itself wings and fly high enough to assume power equal to such a creation? Could spiritual force so far descend or material force so far aspire? Or, when the very stars, and all the armed children of heaven, the "helmed cherubim" that guide and the "sworded seraphim" that guard their several planets, wept for pity and fear at sight of this new force of monstrous matter seen in the deepest night as a fire of menace to man—

[8] London, I, 119.
[9] *A Father's Memoir,* p. xxxvii.

Did he smile his work to see?
. Did he who made the lamb make thee? [10]

By calling the Tyger a "new force of monstrous matter" and "a fire of menace to man," Swinburne distorts the question. He also ignores the typical meaning of stars in Blake's symbolism as well as the significance of a cancelled stanza's being a cancelled stanza. Yeats and Ellis, editors of the first collection of Blake's complete works, take a different view in their brief comment: "The 'Tiger' is, of course, the tiger of wrath, wiser in his own way than the horse of instruction, but always, like the roaring of lions and the destructive sword, so terrible as to be a 'portion of eternity too great for the eye of man.' " [11] S. Foster Damon, in his monumental *William Blake: His Philosophy and Symbols,* first published in 1924, finds the question of the poem to be "how to reconcile the Forgiveness of Sins (the Lamb) with the Punishment of Sins (the Tyger)." The Wrath of the Tyger had to be of divine origin ("His God was essentially personal; therefore Evil must be his Wrath"). The purpose of Wrath is "to consume Error, to annihilate those stubborn beliefs which cannot be removed by the tame 'horses of instruction.' " Yet Damon also thinks that "Did he who made the Lamb make thee?" is "not an exclamation of wonder, but a very real question, whose answer Blake was not sure of." [12]

For Joseph H. Wicksteed, author of the most detailed commentary on the *Songs,* the poem's questions do seem to have a definite answer. "The whole thesis of 'The Tyger,' " he writes, "is that he is a spiritual expression of the Creator himself . . . 'The Tyger' is a tremendous treatise enunciating the nature of the God that *does* exist—the God that is mightily and terribly visible in his manifestations." Attempting to discover the history of Blake's inner life through the visions and revisions of the Notebook, Wicksteed decided that "the composition of this great poem registers (perhaps effects) a change in Blake's mind," carrying him beyond the world view of the *Songs of Experience* to that of the prophecies.[13]

Since the time of these pioneer critics, writers on the poem have

[10] London, 1868, p. 120. For Blake's actual spelling and punctuation, see *The Complete Writings of William Blake,* ed. Geoffrey Keynes (London, 1966), pp. 172, 173, 214. This edition will hereafter be cited as K.

[11] Edwin John Ellis and William Butler Yeats, *The Works of William Blake* (London, 1893), II, 14.

[12] Pp. 277–278.

[13] *Blake's Innocence and Experience* (London, 1928), pp. 196, 212.

continued to disagree about whether the Tyger is "good," created by
the Lamb's creator; ambiguous, its creator unknown and the question
of the poem unanswerable; or "evil," created by some maleficent force.
The first of these views has been given succinct expression by Mark
Schorer:

> The juxtaposition of lamb and tiger points not merely to the opposition
> of innocence and experience, but to the resolution of the paradox they
> present. The innocent impulses of the lamb have been curbed by re-
> straints, and the lamb has turned into something else, indeed into the
> tiger. Innocence is converted to experience. It does not rest there. Energy
> can be curbed but it cannot be destroyed, and when it reaches the limits
> of its endurance, it bursts forth in revolutionary wrath.[14]

Similar to Schorer's interpretation in this respect are those of David V.
Erdman, Stanley Gardner, Martin K. Nurmi, F. W. Bateson, and
Martin Price.[15]

Among those who have seen the Tyger as either ambiguous or
ambivalent are Northrop Frye, Hazard Adams, Robert F. Gleckner,
John E. Grant, Paul Miner, E. D. Hirsch, Jr., and Philip Hobsbaum.
Frye advises the reader of the poem to "leave it a question." Adams,
in his generally valuable essay on "The Tyger," finds two views within
the poem; however, he emphasizes the "visionary" one, according to
which "the tiger symbolizes the primal spiritul energy which may
bring form out of chaos and unite man with that part of his own
being which he has allowed somehow to sleep walk into the dreadful
forests of material darkness." Gleckner, setting "The Tyger" against
some passages in *The Four Zoas,* also finds two views. Grant, in his
finely considered discussion, "The Art and Argument of 'The Tyger,' "
indicates agreement with Wicksteed but, unlike Wicksteed, finds only
conditional answers.

> If he who made the Lamb also made the Tyger, it is because the two
> beasts are contraries. . . . If the creator smiles because he sees that in the
> end the Tyger will leave the forest along with man, a man may feel justi-

[14] *William Blake: The Politics of Vision* (New York, 1946), pp. 250–251.
[15] Erdman, *Blake: Prophet Against Empire* (Princeton, 1954), pp. 179–180. Erdman,
like Schorer, regards the questions of the poem as rhetorical. Gardner, *Infinity on the
Anvil* (Oxford, 1954), pp. 123–130. Nurmi, "Blake's Revisions of *The Tyger*," *PMLA*,
LXXI (1956), 669–685. [An excerpt from this essay is included among the selections in
this volume.] Bateson, *Selected Poems of William Blake,* pp. 117–119. Price, *To the
Palace of Wisdom* (Garden City, N.Y.), 1964, pp. 398–400. [See "The Vision of
Innocence," included among the selections in this volume.]

fied in asking why it is his lot now to be cast among savage beasts. This question cannot be removed from "The Tyger," and, in spite of assertions to the contrary, it was one of the questions which continued to concern Blake throughout his life.

Both Miner and Hirsch find two different perspectives maintained throughout the poem, though they see its final answer as affirmative. Hobsbaum cautions readers against answering the questions, as he regards Blake himself as being in doubt about them.[16]

Two recent commentators on the poem consider the Tyger to be perceived as evil. Harold Bloom regards this perception as the error of the "speaker" of the poem, which he thinks of as a monologue delivered by a Bard in the fallen state of Experience. "The Bard of Experience is in mental darkness . . . The Bard is one of the Redeemed, capable of imaginative salvation, but before the poem ends he has worked his frenzy into the self-enclosure of the Elect Angels, prostrate before a mystery entirely of his own creation." [17] This Bard, whom I cannot help regarding as entirely read into the poem, would resemble Adams' shadowy first speaker, for whom the creator of the Tyger must be a Urizenic God, a "devil-maker." [18] Miss Kathleen Raine, pursuing a different method, comes to a parallel conclusion: that the creator of the Tyger *is* such a devil-maker. She suggests sources in Gnostic and Hermetic mysticism as proof that "the Lamb was made by the son of God, the second person of the Trinity . . . the Tiger was made by the demiurge, the third person of the (Gnostic and Cabbalistic) trinity. Lamb and Tiger inhabit different worlds, and are the work of different creators." To Miss Raine the Tyger seems "a symbol of competitive, predacious selfhood." [19]

The meaning of "The Tyger" has been and continues to be disputed. I would like to suggest that our understanding of the poem can be deepened and enhanced if we regard it against the traditions I have mentioned: that of Jakob Boehme, his predecessor Paracelsus,

[16] Frye, "Blake After Two Centuries," *UTQ*, XXVII (1957), 12. Adams, *William Blake: A Reading of the Shorter Poems* (Seattle, 1963), p. 73. Gleckner, *The Piper & the Bard* (Detroit, 1959), pp. 275–290. [An extract from this book is included among the selections in this volume.] Grant (ed.), *Discussions of William Blake* (Boston, 1961), p. 75. Miner, " 'The Tyger': Genesis and Evolution in the Poetry of William Blake," *Criticism*, IV (1962), 59–73. Hirsch, *Innocence and Experience: An Introduction to Blake* (New Haven, 1964), pp. 244–252. Hobsbaum, "A Rhetorical Question Answered: Blake's Tyger and Its Critics," *Neophilologus*, XLVIII (1964), 151–155.
[17] *Blake's Apocalypse* (Garden City, N.Y., 1963), pp. 137–138.
[18] *William Blake*, p. 65.
[19] "Who Made the Tyger?" *Encounter*, II (1954), 48, 43.

and his disciple William Law; and that of the British theoreticians of
the sublime in the eighteenth century. These disparate traditions have
at least one nexus other than their meeting in the mind of William
Blake: for quite different reasons, the expression of the Wrath of God
in the Bible, particularly in the Old Testament, is of great importance
to each of them. This Biblical material also bears directly on Blake's
theme in "The Tyger." I shall propose that "The Tyger" is an
apostrophe to Wrath as a "sublime" phenomenon, to Wrath both in
the Prophetic sense and as what Boehme calls the First Principle. The
images and rhetoric of the poem will be found to support such an
interpretation.

II

In the Old Testament Prophets, divine wrath is often associated
with a Day of Yahweh which will accomplish the destruction of evil
and establish a community of the righteous. In the later Prophets
"that day" brings about a new earth and a new heaven, sometimes
ruled by the Messiah. Similarly, the manifestation of wrath in Revelation destroys Babylon and is followed by the Parousia and the building of the new Jerusalem. This eschatological wrath, in both the Old
and the New Testaments, frequently appears in the images of fire and
of beasts of prey; sometimes it is represented by both together. Elsewhere, as the echoes of Isaiah in *The Marriage* and in *America* indicate, Blake portrayed the revolutionary events of his day as a fulfill-
ment of this Prophetic vision. A few of many possible examples will
suggest that he also did so in "The Tyger."

In the Prophets' depictions of the Day of Yahweh, the Wrath which
brings on the establishment of the Kingdom is commonly depicted,
as in Blake's poem, as fire:

> For, behold, the Lord will come with fire, and with his chariots like a
> whirlwind, to render his anger with fury, and his rebuke with flames
> of fire.
>
> *(Isaiah* lxvi.15)

> But who may abide the day of his coming? and who shall stand when
> he appeareth? for he is like a refiner's fire, and like fullers' soap.
>
> *(Malachi* iii.2)

Sometimes, once more as in Blake's poem, the image of a forest is
introduced:

Therefore thus saith the Lord God; As the vine tree among the trees of the forest, which I have given to the fire for fuel, so will I give the inhabitants of Jerusalem. And I will set my face against them; they shall go out from one fire, and another fire shall devour them . . .

(Ezekiel xv.6–7)

But I will punish you according to the fruit of your doings, saith the Lord; and I will kindle a fire in the forest thereof, and it shall devour all things round about it.

(Jeremiah xxi.14)[20]

In Amos, we find both the images of the beast of prey and the fire as symbols of God's wrath and coming Judgment:

Will a lion roar in the forest, when he hath no prey?

(iii.4)

The lion hath roared, who will not fear? the Lord God hath spoken, who can but prophesy?

(iii.8)

Seek the Lord, and ye shall live; lest he break out like fire in the house of Joseph, and devour it . . .

(v.6)

In beginning his poem with the Tyger burning bright in the night forests, Blake was using a figurative conception familiar to him in the writings of the Prophets. The allusion is to the Wrath of the Lord burning through the forests of a corrupt social order. To this eschatological conception Blake brings his own doctrine of contraries, partly derived from Boehme.

III

Jakob Boehme and his English disciple William Law occupy an important place in Blake's intellectual biography. "Any man of mechanical talents," Blake said in *The Marriage*, "may, from the writings of Paracelsus or Jacob Behmen, produce ten thousand volumes of equal

---

[20] This passage from Jeremiah is cited in connection with "The Tyger" by Erdman, p. 181 n. A. J. Heschel writes in *The Prophets* (New York and Evanston, 1962, p. 116): "The divine word moved in Jeremiah as fire because he lived through the experience of divine wrath. Just as the pathetic wrath of God could become a physical fire of destruction, so the wrathful word of the prophet could work itself out as a destructive fiery element."

value with Swedenborg's" (K. 158). "Paracelsus & Behmen appear'd
to me," he wrote in describing his "lot in the Heavens" to John Flax-
man (K. 799). Henry Crabb Robinson recalled that Blake called
Boehme "a divinely inspired man." "Bl praised too the figures in Law's
transln. as being very beautiful. Mich. Angelo cod. not have done
better." [21] One of the seminal ideas that Blake derived from Boehme
is that God manifests Himself in two contrary principles: Wrath and
Love, Fire and Light, Father and Son. These principles are not
dualistically opposed: they are contraries in an unending dialectic
whose synthesis is the Godhead. As I think this conception is of great
importance to an understanding of Blake's thought, I shall quote at
some length from Boehme. Reference is to the "Law translation,"
which is really an edition made up by Law and his followers.

> As God the Father himself is *All;* he is the Number Three of the Deity;
> he is the Majesty; he is the still Eternity; he is the Nature, and in it he
> is the Love and the Anger: the Anger is a cause of his Strength and
> Might; as also a cause of Life, and of all Mobility, as the Poison [or
> Gall] in Man is: and the Love is a cause of the Heart of his Majesty, and
> a cause of the Number Three, and of the Three Principles.

> the Fire is a cause of the Light, for without fire there would be no Light,
> so there would be no *Love* without Light; the Light is Love . . . and we
> see that the Light and the fire have *two several* [properties or] sources;
> the *fire* is biting, wrathful, devouring and consuming; and the *Light* is
> pleasant, sweet, and desirous of a Body; the Love desireth a Body; and
> the fire also desireth a Body for its nourishment, but devoureth it quite;
> and the Light raiseth it up, and desireth to fill it; it taketh nothing away
> from the Body, but quickens it, and makes it friendly.

> Thus we may consider with ourselves, *whence* it ariseth that there is a
> wrathful and a good will: For you see the Fire hath *two* Spirits, *one* is
> that which proceedeth from the Heat, and the other that which pro-
> ceedeth from the Light: Now the Heat is Nature, and the Light is the
> Eternal Liberty without [or beyond] Nature: for Nature comprehendeth
> not the Light.

> And so you must understand us concerning the *two* sorts of wills in
> God, the *one* is Nature, and is not called God, and yet is God's, for he is
> angry, severe, sharp as a sting, consuming, attracting all things to himself,

[21] *Blake, Coleridge, Wordsworth, Lamb, Etc.,* ed. Edith J. Morley (Manchester and
London, 1922), p. 6.

and devouring them, always striving, to fly up above the Light, [which is the *other* will,] and yet cannot.[22]

A flame represents the inter-action and inter-dependence of the two wills, its light corresponding to God's Love, its heat to His Wrath.

> And yet the Fire gives or represents to us a *Mystery* of the eternal Nature, and of the Deity also, wherein a Man is to understand two Principles of a twofold Source, *viz.* I. a hot, fierce, astringent, bitter, anxious, consuming One in the Fire-source. And out of the Fire comes the II *viz.* the Light, which dwells in the Fire, but is not apprehended or laid hold on by the Fire; also it has another Source than the Fire has, which is *Meekness,* wherein there is a Desire of *Love,* where then, in the Love-desire, another Will is understood than that which the Fire has.[23]

Law is at least as explicit on the mutual dependence of the two wills and their ultimate unity:

> the Father has His distinct manifestation in the fire, which is always generating the light; the Son has His distinct manifestation in the light, which is always generated from the fire; the Holy Ghost has His manifestation in the spirit, that always proceeds from both, and is always united with them.[24]

Blake gave pictorial expression to the Two Principles in his allegorical illustration of James Hervey's *Meditations Among the Tombs.*[25] In one corner of the painting, to the left of God the Father, Blake wrote "Wrath"; in the other corner, "Mercy"; and directly to the left of God, "God out of Christ is a Consuming Fire." This again suggests that Blake characteristically thought of Wrath in Boehme's sense, for in *Aurora,* 14, #49, we find: "But in the Outspeaking of his Word, wherein the Nature of the spiritual World exists . . . and wherein *God calls himself an angry,* zealous or *jealous God and a consuming Fire,* therein . . . indeed God *has known the Evil* from Eternity . . . but therein is he *not called God,* but a consuming Fire."

The Two Principles are analogous to Blake's contrary states of Innocence and Experience. Meekness is apposite to the visionary poet in

---

[22] *The Threefold Life of Man,* Part 7, sections 62, 63, 65, 66; *The Works of Jacob Behmen, the Teutonic Theosopher* (London, 1764–81), II, 76.

[23] *Aurora,* Part 11, section 92, *Works of Jacob Behmen,* I, 99.

[24] "An Appeal," *Selected Mystical Writings of William Law,* ed. Stephen Hobhouse (New York, 1948), p. 46.

[25] The picture is reproduced in Damon's *A Blake Dictionary* (Providence, R.I., 1965), Pl. XI; Damon's interesting descriptive commentary is on pp. 183–184.

one State, Wrath in the other.[26] The poet of Experience must endeavor, like Boehme and Law, to show that Wrath is the self-executing judgment of God in a fallen world. By doing so, he will pass "beyond" Experience into inspired prophecy. The Tyger shows the way to this, embodying the Wrath of the First Principle unfolded in history as the great human upheaval of the French Revolution. Angels call it evil. The poet aspiring toward prophecy perceives and fixes its terrible energies as sublime.

IV

Terror, in the eighteenth century, was commonly considered the highest manifestation of sublimity. "Indeed," wrote Burke, "terror is in all cases whatsoever, either more openly or latently the ruling principle of the sublime." [27] Dennis had tried to explain why this was so.

the Care, which Nature has inrooted in all, of their own Preservation, is the Cause that Men are unavoidably terrify'd with any thing that threatens approaching Evil. 'Tis now our Business to shew how the Ideas of Serpents, Lions, Tygers, &c. were made by the Art of those great Poets, to be terrible to their Readers, at the same time that we are secure from their Objects.[28]

Burke's psychological explanation follows Dennis':

Whatever is fitted in any sort to excite the ideas of pain, and danger, that is to say, whatever is in any sort terrible, or is conversant about terrible objects, or operates in a manner analogous to terror, is a source of the *sublime;* that is, it is productive of the strongest emotion which the mind is capable of feeling.[29]

The chief effect of the sublime is "astonishment"—"that state of the soul, in which all its motions are suspended, with some degree of horror," and "the mind is so entirely filled with its object, that it

[26] I should note that Gerald E. Bentley, Jr., suggests, without going further into this subject, that "The question of 'The Tyger' is whether the wrath principle and the love principle emanate from the same eternal being."—"William Blake and the Alchemical Philosophers," diss. (Merton College, Oxford, 1954), p. 216.
[27] *Enquiry into the Origin of Our Ideas of the Sublime and Beautiful*, ed. J. T. Boulton (London, 1958), p. 58.
[28] *The Grounds of Criticism in Poetry*, in *The Critical Works of John Dennis*, ed. Edward Niles Hooker (Baltimore, Md., 1939), I, 362.
[29] *Enquiry*, p. 39.

cannot entertain any other, nor by consequence reason on that object which employs it" (p. 57). These effects are produced when we contemplate dangerous objects which we know cannot harm us. Like Dennis, Burke finds examples of this which bring Blake's poem to mind: "We have continually about us animals of a strength that is considerable, but not pernicious. Amongst these we never look for the sublime: it comes upon us in the gloomy forest, and in the howling wilderness, in the form of the lion, the tiger, the panther, or rhinoceros" (p. 66).

For these writers the chief examples of the sublime in literature were to be found in the Old Testament,[30] which they found particularly rich in the sublime of terror:

> Now of all these Ideas none are so terrible as those which shew the Wrath and Vengeance of an angry God; for nothing is so wonderful in its Effects: and consequently the Images or Ideas of those Effects must carry a great deal of Terror with them, which we may see was *Longinus's* Opinion, by the Examples which he brings in his Chapter of the Sublimity of the Thoughts.[31]

Dennis goes on to produce examples of Wrath from Habbakuk and Psalms, comparing them with passages from Homer to the advantage of the former (pp. 366–368). Lowth writes, in a similar vein:

> Nothing, however, can be greater or more magnificent than the representation of anger and indignation, particularly when the Divine wrath is displayed. Of this the whole of the prophetic Song of Moses affords an incomparable specimen [Cites Deut. xxxii.40–42, followed by Is. lxiii.4–6] . . . The display of the fury and threats of the enemy, by which Moses finely exaggerates the horror of their unexpected ruin, is also wonderfully sublime. [Cites Ex. xv.9–10][32]

Of the Biblical passages which Dennis, Lowth, Burke, and others display as instances of the sublime, many have in common with Blake's poem the depiction of wrath in terms of fire, beasts of prey, or both. Lowth, for example, comments on

> the sublimity of those passages . . . in which the image is taken from the roaring of a lion, the clamour of rustic labourers, and the rage of wild beasts:

[30] See Samuel H. Monk, *The Sublime: A Study of Critical Theories in XVIII-Century England* (Ann Arbor, Mich., 1960), pp. 79–80.
[31] Dennis, *Grounds of Criticism*, p. 361.
[32] Robert Lowth, *Lectures on the Sacred Poetry of the Hebrews* (London, 1787), I, 379–381.

Jehovah from on high shall roar,
And from his holy habitation shall he utter his voice;
He shall roar aloud against his resting-place,
A shout like that of the vintagers shall he give
Against all the inhabitants of the earth.

And I will be unto them as a lion;
As a leopard in the way will I watch them:
I will meet them as a bear bereaved of her whelps:
And I will rend the caul of their heart:
And there will I devour them as a lioness;
A beast of the field shall tear them.[33]

William Smith, in the notes to his translation of Longinus, gave a number of examples of sublimity, among them this passage from Psalm xviii: "There went up a smoke out of his nostrils, and fire out of his mouth devoured: coals were kindled at it . . . And he rode upon a Cherub, and did fly, and came flying upon the wings of the wind." [34] "The Sublime of the Bible," as Blake calls it in *Milton* (K. 480), was an established critical doctrine,[35] and the most powerful manifestations of such sublimity were in descriptions of divine wrath and power. The single book of the Bible which was considered most sublime in the eighteenth century, and which was also to be the subject of Blake's great pictorial interpretation in old age, was Job. Lowth declared of the book as a whole: "Not only the force, the beauty, the sublimity of the sentiments are unrivalled; but such is the character of the diction in general, so vivid is the expression, so interesting the assemblage of objects, so close and connected the sentences, so animated and passionate the whole arrangement, that the Hebrew literature itself contains nothing more poetical" (I, 313). Almost all of Lowth's Lecture xiv, "Of the Sublime in General," is devoted to Job, in addition to three lectures on the work itself. Burke (p. 63) found Job iv. 13–17 "a passage amazingly sublime . . . principally due to the terrible uncertainty of the thing described." The same passage served Smith (p. 152) as an example of the sublime of horror, and Blake used part of it as the theme for his ninth illustration to Job—"Then a Spirit passed before my face: the hair of my flesh stood up.

---

[33] I, 363. Jer. xxv.30, Hos. xiii.7, 8. My own Biblical citations are from the Authorized Version, but in an instance such as this one where the author provides his own translation, I reproduce the text as he gives it, unless otherwise noted.

[34] *Dionysius Longinus on the Sublime* (London, 1743), p. 127.

[35] Cf. Coleridge's "Sublimity is Hebrew by birth," quoted by Monk, p. 79 n.

. . . Shall mortal Man be more just than God?" Section v of Burke's *Enquiry,* "Power," draws numerous examples of its subject from Job. Among these are the descriptions of Behemoth and Leviathan, symbolic beasts to which the Tyger is related as an embodiment of sublime power.

In his later writings and paintings, Blake portrays Leviathan as a demonic parody of the sublime, but this change in his symbolism, reflecting his changed view of revolution after the rise of Napoleon, occurred long after "The Tyger" was written. To ignore this fact in linking Tyger and Leviathan (as Bloom does, p. 138) is to distort the meaning of the poem. At this point we should rather think of the tiger-striped Leviathan of *The Marriage of Heaven and Hell,* which advances (from the direction of Paris)[36] "with all the fury of a spiritual existence" (K. 156). The Tyger is like the Leviathan of Job in that both are fiery images of divine energy:

> Out of his mouth go burning lamps, and sparks of fire leap out.
> Out of his nostrils goeth smoke, as out of a seething pot or caldron.
> His breath kindleth coals, and a flame goeth out of his mouth.
> In his neck remaineth strength, and sorrow is turned into joy before him.

> (xli.19–22)

Such power cannot be explained; it can only be evoked, as by the questions which the Lord asks Job from the whirlwind, or by those which Blake's speaker asks in "The Tyger." [37] "Did he who made the Lamb make thee?" no more demands an explicit answer than "Who hath divided a watercourse for the overflowing of the waters, or a way for the lightning of thunder?" Leviathan is the culminating image of God's speech to Job because as an embodiment of power it completes the process of raising the Job problem out of the realm of ethical discourse, inducing an attitude of awe, wonder, and astonishment which the eighteenth century called sublime. This is the function of "The Tyger" in the *Songs of Experience.*

V

"The Tyger"

Tyger! Tyger! burning bright
In the forests of the night,

---

[36] See Nurmi, p. 671 n.
[37] Erdman suggests a possible indirect connection between the two through a paraphrase in James Hervey's *Theron and Aspasio* (1775)—*Blake,* p. 103.

> What immortal hand or eye
> Could frame thy fearful symmetry?
>
> In what distant deeps or skies
> Burnt the fire of thine eyes?
> On what wings dare he aspire?
> What the hand dare seize the fire?
>
> And what shoulder, & what art
> Could twist the sinews of thy heart?
> And when thy heart began to beat,
> What dread hand? & what dread feet?
>
> What the hammer? what the chain?
> In what furnace was thy brain?
> What the anvil? what dread grasp
> Dare its deadly terrors clasp?
>
> When the stars threw down their spears,
> And water'd heaven with their tears,
> Did he smile his work to see?
> Did he who made the Lamb make thee?
>
> Tyger! Tyger! burning bright
> In the forests of the night,
> What immortal hand or eye
> Dare frame thy fearful symmetry? [38]

Our contemporary reader would have seen the sublimity of "The Tyger" not only in its theme but in its rhetoric and imagery as well. First there are the questions of which Blake's poem entirely consists, and which I have compared to those of Job: in both cases sublimity lies in the form as well as in the content. For example, Edward Young wrote in a note to his own verse paraphrase of Job: "*Longinus* has a chapter on interrogations, which shews that they contribute much to the sublime. This speech of the Almighty is made up of them." [39] Smith, commenting on that same chapter (xviii) in Longinus, remarked: "To these Instances may be added the whole 38th Chapter

---

[38] K. 214. In one copy of the *Songs*, l. 12 was altered to "What dread hand Form'd thy dread feet?" (Copy P, in Geoffrey Keynes and Edwin Wolf, *William Blake's Illuminated Books: A Census*, New York, 1953, p. 61). Malkin printed the line as "What dread hand forged thy dread feet?" Damon, *William Blake*, p. 279, thinks this emendation was Blake's own. Bateson, *Selected Poems*, p. 118, notes that "forged" is the reading in Wordsworth's Commonplace Book.

[39] *The Works of the Author of the Night-Thoughts* (London, 1792), I, 188 n. See also Lowth, I, 357.

of Job; where we behold the Almighty Creator expostulating with his Creature. . . . There we see how vastly useful the Figure of Interrogation is, in giving us a lofty Idea of the Deity, whilst every Question awes us into Silence, and inspires a Sense of our own Insufficiency" (p. 155). Blake's poem has other sublime elements as well. Richard Hurd associated sublimity with "apostrophes and invocations" [40]— "The Tyger" is, of course, both. (Hurd also wrote that poetry "calls up infernal spectres to terrify, or brings down celestial natures to astonish, the imagination.") As for diction, Blake's exhibits the qualities which Lowth praised in Hebrew poetry—"sparing in words, concise, and energetic" (ii, 250). One could easily apply to "The Tyger" the statement that "The sublimity of the matter is perfectly equalled by the unaffected energy of the style" (ii, 251); Lowth is speaking of Psalm xxix, in which "The voice of the Lord divideth the flames of fire. The voice of the Lord shaketh the wilderness; the Lord shaketh the wilderness of Kadesh" (7–8, A.V.). Such a comparison was made more or less explicitly by Malkin, who in discussing Blake's *Songs* observed "The devotional pieces of the Hebrew bards are clothed in that simple language, to which Johnson with justice ascribes the character of sublimity" (p. xxxi). Among later writers on the poem, only Gilchrist made use of this hint. Also, in addition to being simple and energetic, Blake's diction employs what Professor Miles (p. 57) so aptly calls the "vocabulary of cosmic passion and sense impression" which characterizes the sublime poem of the late eighteenth century. Vistas open in "distant deeps or skies," penetrated by the "immortal hand or eye" of a being who dares "aspire" on "wings"; "the stars" and "heaven" participate in the cosmic drama. Other expressions, in stanzas three and four, belong to the vocabulary of the sublime of terror: "dread hand," "dread feet," "dread grasp," and "deadly terrors." In his use of sublime language, as Professor Miles has demonstrated, Blake is very much a poet of his era.

Having discussed the sublimity of "The Tyger," we must turn to the symbolic meanings which its images represent. It is here, of course, that Blake differs from poets who merely imitated the Bible. Blake's images have meanings which may in part be construed from the internal logic of the poem, but which also depend at least in part upon meanings established elsewhere, in Blake's other poems or in the

---

[40] Quoted by Josephine Miles in *Eras and Modes in English Poetry* (Berkeley and Los Angeles, 1964), p. 66; from *On the Idea of Universal Poetry, The Works of Richard Hurd, D.D.*, ii (London, 1811), 9.

traditional sources from which he drew. We learn to understand
Blake's forests, tears, fire, stars, and furnaces as we do Shelley's veils,
boats, rivers, and caves, or Yeats's spindles and swans. Meaning is
affected by context, though not entirely determined by it. Fire, for
example, has a different significance for Blake when it gives both heat
and light than when it gives heat alone, and furnaces may be creative
or destructive, depending on what is going on in them. In interpreting
these images, we must beware of assigning sources too narrowly, or of
mechanically transferring a meaning from one context to an entirely
different one. We should, instead, try to understand what each image
contributes to the effect of the poem as a whole.

The Tyger embodies the *contrarium* of Wrath in the Godhead,
"Burning bright" with Prophetic fire and perceived as a sublime
phenomenon. He is God's judgment upon the world of Experience.
In Blake's Notebook he appears after the moral terrain of that world
has been charted in terms of the hapless soldier, the blackening church,
the harlot, the chimney sweep. This debased and corrupt order produces a contrary to the Lamb of Innocence in the Tyger. But Contraries are not Negations. The Tyger is not "a symbol of competitive,
predacious selfhood." Wrath is a vice only in the unfallen world of
Innocence; in our world, in the London or Paris of 1792, Mercy and
the other virtues of Innocence are vices.

> I heard an Angel singing
> When the day was springing,
> "Mercy, Pity, Peace
> "Is the world's release."
>
> Thus he sung all day
> Over the new mown hay,
> Till the sun went down
> And haycocks looked brown.
>
> I heard a Devil curse
> Over the heath & the furze
> "Mercy could be no more,
> "If there was nobody poor,
>
> "And pity no more could be,
> "If all were happy as we."
> At his curse the sun went down,
> And the heavens gave a frown.

> And Miseries' increase
> Is Mercy, Pity, Peace.[41]

The Tyger, ultimate product of Experience, shows the way out of Experience to the earthly paradise of *The Marriage of Heaven and Hell*:

> Then the perilous path was planted,
> And a river and a spring
> On every cliff and tomb,
> And on the bleached bones
> Red clay brought forth

But man's attempt to create such a paradise on earth came in the bloody aspect of the French Revolution. "One might as well think of establishing a republic of tigers in some forest of Africa," [42] declared Sir Samuel Romilly after the September Massacres, and Wordsworth in the fall of 1792 found Revolutionary Paris

> a place of fear
> Unfit for the repose which night requires,
> Defenceless as a wood where tigers roam.[43]

In *The Book of Ahania* (1795), where the energy principle temporarily overthrows repressive reason, "Fuzon, his tygers unloosing, / Thought Urizen slain by his wrath." [44] The image of the tiger seems to have been almost inevitable.

Night, forests, and stars are frequently used by Blake as symbols of the old order, *l'épaisse nuit gothique* of Holy Europe. "Thy Nobles have gather'd thy starry hosts round this rebellious city," declares the warlike Burgundy to the King in *The French Revolution* (1791), "To rouze up the ancient forests of Europe with clarions of cloud [loud?] breathing war" (ll. 100–101). He fears that the revolutionaries will "mow down all this great starry harvest of six thousand years" (l. 90) and that "the ancient forests of chivalry" will be "hewn" (l. 93). In the same poem, Orleans, speaking for the popular cause, talks of "the wild raging millions, that wander in forests, and howl in law blasted wastes"

[41] K. 164 ("Poems from the Note-Book 1793"). Deleted lines omitted.

[42] Quoted by Asa Briggs in *The Age of Improvement* (London, 1960), pp. 134–135.

[43] *The Prelude* (1805), ed. Ernest de Selincourt (Oxford, 1959), p. 370. For the date of composition of "The Tyger" (fall of 1792), see Erdman, pp. 167 n. and 174; Nurmi, p. 671 n.

[44] See my "Method and Meaning in Blake's *Book of Ahania*," *BNYPL*, LXX (1966), 27–33.

(l. 227). This is similar, too, to "The Argument" of *The Marriage of Heaven and Hell,* where "the just man rages in the wilds / Where lions roam" (K. 149). In *Europe* (1794), "The night of Nature" is eighteen centuries of history which culminate in the war of 1793, when "The Tigers couch upon the prey & suck the ruddy tide" (K. 245). In the same poem man enmeshed in material error hides "In forests of night" (K. 241). There is, perhaps, a suggestion of Dante's *selva oscura* in the image, and of Spenser's Wood of Error. It may also recall Thomas Taylor's use of woods as a symbol of material nature,[45] and, as was pointed out earlier, the Prophets sometimes use the forest to stand for the corrupt order which God will burn. Blake need not have consciously borrowed his forest symbol from any of these sources to have been aware of its meanings in them. Such awareness, together with a feeling of affinity, influences the conceptions of a poet and makes traditional symbols viable in his work, as we see again in Blake's use of the stars.

Lines 17–18 have several related meanings. The literal image is of starlight and dew; Frederick Pottle suggests "When the stars faded out in the dawn and the dew fell." [46] On the historical level, the stars represent the armies of monarchy; as early as the *Poetical Sketches* and as late as *Jerusalem,* Blake associates the stars with tyranny and war:

> The stars of heaven tremble; the roaring voice of war,
> the trumpet, calls to battle!
>
> ("Prologue to King John," K. 34)

> Loud the Sun & Moon rage in the conflict: loud the Stars
> Shout in the night of battle, & their spears grow to their hands,
> With blood weaving the deaths of the Mighty into a Tabernacle
> For Rahab & Tirzah, till the Great Polypus of Generation
> covered the Earth.
>
> (*Jerusalem,* 61: 31–34, K. 704) [47]

---

[45] "But when he [Virgil, in *Aeneid* VI] says that all the middle regions are covered with woods, this likewise plainly intimates a material nature . . ."—*The Eleusinian and Bacchic Mysteries* (New York, 1875), p. 20. See George Mills Harper. *The Neoplatonism of William Blake* (Chapel Hill, N.C., 1961), pp. 157 and 169.

[46] *Explicator,* VIII (1950), #39.

[47] Cf. *Jerusalem,* 55: 27, where "The Stars in their courses fought," (K. 686), echoing Judges v.20. Several lines after this, the Eternals name the Eighth Eye of God, but "he came not, he hid in Albion's Forests" (33). In this later phase of his thought, Blake believes that the destructive wrath of revolution should be restrained; therefore the Words of the Eternals are described as "Curbing their Tygers with golden bits & bridles of silver & ivory" (35).

"The stars threw down their spears" appears in Night v of *The Four Zoas,* where, as Erdman points out, Urizen's words refer to the defeat of the counter-revolutionary armies at Yorktown and Valmy:

> "I call'd the stars around my feet in the night of councils, dark;
> The stars threw down their spears & fled naked away.
> We fell . . ." [48]

(Also compare the defeat of the British as described in *America,* 15: 4–5: "The millions sent up a howl of anguish and threw off their hammer'd mail, / And cast their swords & spears to earth, & stood, a naked multitude.") The meaning of Blake's stars derives in part from Revelation. In xii.4 the stars are Satan's legions: "And his tail drew the third part of the stars of heaven, and did cast them to the earth"; while in the apocalypse of Chapter vi, after the Lamb of God opens the sixth seal, "the stars of heaven fell unto the earth, even as a fig tree casteth her untimely figs, when she is shaken of a mighty wind" (13). Coleridge, who like Blake saw the French Revolution as an apocalyptic event, uses this latter image in *Religious Musings:*

> And lo! the Great, the Rich, the Mighty Men,
> The Kings and the Chief Captains of the World,
> With all that fixed on high like stars of Heaven
> Shot baleful influence, shall be cast to earth[49]

"This passage," Coleridge noted (p. 121), "alludes to the French Revolution. . . . I am convinced that the Babylon of the Apocalypse does not apply to Rome exclusively; but to the union of Religion with Power and Wealth, wherever it is found," a statement which could have been made by Blake as well. Revelation vi ends, significantly, "For the great day of his wrath is come; and who shall be able to stand?" (17).

Blake also thought of the stars as symbols of oppression because they were associated both with the mechanism of the Newtonian universe and with the instrumentality of fate. The defeat of the stars signifies the casting off of both cosmic and internal constraint, freeing man to realize his potentially divine nature. This is also a theme in Paracelsus and Boehme. Boehme wrote:

For *the outward life* is fallen quite under the power of the Stars, and if

---

[48] K. 311. See Erdman, p. 178.
[49] Written in 1794. *The Complete Poetical Works of Samuel Taylor Coleridge,* ed. Ernest Hartley Coleridge (Oxford, 1912), I, 121.

thou wilt withstand them, thou must enter into God's will, and then they
are but as a shadow, and cannot bring that to effect which they have in
their power: *neither do they desire it,* but the Devil only desireth it:
For the whole Nature boweth itself before the will of God: For the
Image of God in Man is so powerful and mighty, that when it wholly
casteth itself into the will of God, it overpowereth Nature, so that the
Stars are *obedient* to it, and do rejoice themselves in the Image: for
their will is that they may be freed from the vanity, and thus are kindled
in Meekness in the Image, at which the Heaven rejoiceth, and so the
Anger of God in the Government of this world is *quenched;* for when
that is burning, Man's wickedness is guilty of it, in that Men kindle it
in the Spirit of this world. (*Threefold Life,* Part II, section 38, *Works,*
II, 116)

According to Paracelsus:

The stars are subject to the philosopher, they must follow him, and
not he them. Only the man who is still animal is governed, mastered,
compelled, and driven by the stars, so that he has no choice but to follow
them. . . . But the reason for all this is that such a man does not know
himself and does not know how to use the energies hidden in him, nor
does he know that he carries the stars within himself . . . and thus
carries in him the whole firmament, with all its influences.[50]

After the failure of the Peasants' Revolt, Paracelsus declared: "The
peasants have submitted to the stars, and have been beaten by them.
Whoever trusts the stars, trusts a traitor." [51] In "The Tyger," the
opposite happens: the stars are beaten and desert their order. Man's
fate suddenly becomes of his own making, and the "just man" of "The
Argument" can create a human society, symbolized by the covering of
the bleached bones of the Old Adam with the red clay of the New.

The weeping stars of Blake's poem owe something perhaps to the
anonymous lyric "Tom of Bedlam," reprinted in Joseph Ritson's
Ancient Songs of 1790:

> I behold the stars
> At mortal wars,
> In the wounded welkin weeping

The tears in Blake's poem are doubtless the "tears such as Angels
weep" in *Paradise Lost* 1.620,[52] but of Angels in the Blakean sense—

---

[50] *Selected Writings,* ed. Jolande Jacobi (New York, 1958), p. 154.
[51] Quoted in Henry M. Pachter, *Paracelsus: Magic Into Science* (New York, 1957),
p. 107.
[52] *The Works of John Milton,* ed. Frank Allen Patterson (New York, 1931), II, i, 30.

they are tears of frustration, hypocrisy, repression. This is the burden of meaning carried by tears in other *Songs of Experience*. In "The Human Abstract," Cruelty "waters the ground with tears" in order to make the Tree of Mystery grow. The speaker of "The Angel" (K. 213–214) uses tears as a defense against feeling:

> And I wept both night and day,
> And he wip'd my tears away,
> And I wept both day and night,
> And hid from him my heart's delight.
>
> So he took his wings and fled;
> Then the morn blush'd rosy red;
> I dried my tears, & arm'd my fears
> With ten thousand shields and spears.

In the Lambeth prophecies, Urizen is often depicted as weeping because life cannot keep his iron laws. "And he wept & he called it Pity, / And his tears flowed down on the winds" (*Book of Urizen*, K. 235). Pity, as I have said, is a vice in the world of Experience. It is the error of La Fayette in the poem Blake wrote about him not long after "The Tyger":

> Fayette beheld the King & Queen
> In curses & iron bound;
> But mute Fayette wept tear for tear,
> And guarded them around.
>
> (K. 186)

Erdman suggests a parallel to this in Paine's condemnation of Burke's pity for Marie Antoinette—"He pities the plumage, but forgets the dying bird." [53] If the just man is to find his way out of the forest around him, he must give over his modest stillness and humility and imitate the action of the tiger.

Having discussed the tiger-fire images in the poem and the stars-forest-tears constellation, we must now turn to the third important group of images, those concerned with metalworking.

> What the hammer? what the chain?
> In what furnace was thy brain?
> What the anvil? what dread grasp
> Dare its deadly terrors clasp?

[53] P. 168, from *Rights of Man* (London, 1791), 4th ed., p. 26.

These instruments—hammer, chain, furnace, and anvil—are in Blake's prophetic writings assigned to Los, Eternal Prophet, and symbol of the Imagination.[54] It is the function of Los to create the imaginative constructs which give form to human perception. On plate 6 of *Jerusalem* he is pictured with all four instruments mentioned in "The Tyger," and in *The Book of Los* (1795, K. 260) he forges the sun with them.

> 5. Roaring indignant, the bright sparks
> Endur'd the vast Hammer; but unwearied
> Los beat on the Anvil, till glorious
> An immense Orb of fire he fram'd.
>
> 6. Oft he quench'd it beneath in the Deeps,
> Then survey'd the all bright mass, Again
> Siezing fires from the terrific Orbs,
> He heated the round Globe, then beat,
> While, roaring, his Furnaces endur'd
> The chain'd Orb in their infinite wombs.[55]

The furnace in which the energy-symbols of Sun and Tyger are created is the prophetic imagination: the Hammer is the divine Word. The meanings of these images are supported by, though they do not depend on, their use in the Bible, Paracelsus, and Boehme. In Ezekiel xxii.17–22, the furnace is a simile for the wrath of God:

And the word of the Lord came unto me, saying,

Son of man, the house of Israel is to me become dross: all they are brass, and tin, and iron, and lead, in the midst of the furnace; they are even the dross of silver.

Therefore thus saith the Lord GOD; Because ye are all become dross, behold, therefore I will gather you into the midst of Jerusalem.

As they gather silver, and brass, and iron, and lead, and tin, into the midst of the furnace, to blow the fire upon it, to melt it; so will I gather you in mine anger and in my fury, and I will leave you there, and melt you.

Yea, I will gather you, and blow upon you in the fire of my wrath, and ye shall be melted in the midst thereof.

[54] As noted by Hazard Adams, *Blake and Yeats: The Contrary Vision* (Ithaca, N.Y.), p. 238.

[55] This similarity is discussed in my Brown Univ. master's thesis, "William Blake's Revolutionary Symbolism" (1957), p. 7, and in Miner, " 'The Tyger,' " pp. 67–68.

As silver is melted in the midst of the furnace, so shall ye be melted in the midst thereof; and ye shall know that I the Lord have poured out my fury upon you.

But the furnace does more than melt down; it also purifies: "Behold, I have refined thee, but not with silver; I have chosen thee in the furnace of affliction" (Isaiah xlviii.10). The furnace can be creative as well as destructive, as we see in Psalm xii—"The words of the Lord are pure words: as silver tried in a furnace of earth, purified seven times." The destructive fire of wrath is also the energy of purification. Paracelsus, who believes that destruction perfects that which is good, regards the work of the alchemist's furnace as analogous to this divine activity: "For in the same way as God created the heaven and the earth, the furnace with its fire must be constructed and regulated." "But the sun receives light from no other source than God Himself, Who rules it, so that in the sun God Himself is burning and shining. Just so it is with this Art. The fire in the furnace may be compared to the sun. It heats the furnace and the vessels, just as the sun heats the vast universe. For as nothing can be produced in the world without the sun, so . . . nothing can be produced without this simple fire." [56] Blake carries the alchemical analogy into symbolism—the imaginative activity of the poet-prophet in raising the perceptions of mankind is, metaphorically, the Great Work of turning base metals into gold. Blake's furnace is a perpetual source of power for transforming a dead world. The Hammer, the active force of the *Logos,* beats out the changes. "Is not my word like as a fire? saith the Lord; and like a hammer that breaketh the rock in pieces?" (Jeremiah xxiii.29). Boehme speaks of the Spirit of God as "the right Hammer" which strikes in the soul and makes it long for the love of God. "Such a soul is *easy* to be awakened . . . especially when the Hammer of the Holy Ghost sounds through the Ears into the Heart, then the tincture of the soul receives it *instantly;* and there it goes forth through the whole soul." [57] As if in answer to the closing questions of "The Tyger," in *Jerusalem,* plate 73, all things are created in Los's furnaces, including "the tyger" and "the wooly lamb" (K. 713); and in *The Book of Los,* after creating the sun, "Los smiled with joy" (K. 260).

I do not suggest that we must literally find answers to the questions

[56] "Concerning the Spirits of the Planets," *The Hermetic and Alchemical Writings of Paracelsus,* ed. A. E. Waite (London, 1894), I, 85, 74.
[57] *The Threefold Life of Man,* 1849, p. 194.

of Blake's poem in his sources or in his other writings. What these materials can do is reinforce and corroborate our sense of what the poem means; they also indicate the place of "The Tyger" in Blake's thought. Here the significance of Los as creator is especially important: the Tyger is, to adapt Coleridge's phrase, an educt of the prophetic imagination. Incarnating divine Wrath, it calls to mind the Prophets' representations of God as a beast of prey, the Greyhound of Virgil's prophecy in Canto i of the *Inferno,* and the Lion of the tribe of Juda in Revelation v.5.[58] Its fearful symmetry derives from the dialectical tension of Boehme's First and Second Principles. It inaugurates a Day of Wrath in which man will be tried by fire, but its ultimate function is to create a world in which Innocence will be possible. Those who follow vision through the fallen word of Experience, like the parents of "The Little Girl Found," will discover this.

> Then they followed
> Where the vision led,
> And saw their sleeping child
> Among tygers wild.

How this can be, how (not whether) the Tyger of Wrath can have the same origin as the Lamb of Love, is what Blake's poem asks. The "answer" does not lie with the horses of instruction who vindicate the ways of God to man. Through its imagery and language, with their traditional associations, "The Tyger" leads the responsive reader to an experience of the sublime.

---

[58] Cf. the "Christ the tiger" of Eliot's "Gerontion," in which several other lines also recall Blake:

> Virtues
> Are forced upon us by our impudent crimes.
> These tears are shaken from the wrath-bearing tree.

> The tiger springs in the new year. Us he devours.

PART TWO

View Points

Joseph H. Wicksteed: The Blossom

We are already half way to understanding these two curious little verses.[1] A poem that seems at first a fanciful little garden-song without much meaning, and then a cradle-song in which the mother calls her babe a sparrow when it is happy, and a robin (to rhyme with sobbin'), when it is tearful, is in fact the supreme passage song between the Two Contrary States of the Human Soul. The merry sparrow, like the first laughter of the child in the "Piper," symbolises Innocence, and the sobbing Robin, like the child's tears, symbolises Experience rather than grief. The Little Boy was "found" in the first experience of his own Thought.[2] The Girl "blossoms" into experience through consummated love.

But there was nothing for Blake which Art might not touch. The spirituality which made him call the body "a portion of Soul" gives him the simplicity and frankness of archaic thought, and as the bud and flower in the previous design illustrated the unopened and the opened womb, so this illustration is a poetic and symbolic rendering of the phallus prone and erect, a pillar of vegetable flame breaking at the crest into multitudinous life of many happy spirits, one of which finds its home in the lap of the happy mother, winged for a reason we shall see.

In the poem three out of the six lines in each verse are the same, and it is these that describe the maiden in her moment of earthly beatitude. In the second line "leaves so green" describes the body in its vernal beauty. The third line speaks a joy which does not change as the great passage is effected in the second verse. She is still, in her

"The Blossom," from the book, Blake's Innocence and Experience, *by Joseph H. Wicksteed. Published by E. P. Dutton & Co., Inc., and reprinted with their permission.*

[1] Mr. Damon, who is a very honest as well as a very learned and able Blake scholar, thought so little of this poem that he suggested Blake only kept it in his book because of the beauty of the illustration. He has since confessed his persuasion that the interpretation here given is "quite certainly right," though it was not till he considered the illustration that conviction dawned.

[2] *Cf.* ". . . think not for themselves till Experience teaches them . . . ," and *supra,* Preface, p. 39; also p. 282.

"Experience," "a happy Blossom." The last line in each verse introduces the magic word "My," than which no other word can speak the intensely personal quality of love's moment.

The birds are the male element as seen by the maiden. They represent the whole range of the lover's love, from the winged thought to the accomplished act. In the sacred chamber of the annunciation it will be remembered that the angel of "holy Generation" was endowed with the symbolic wings of a butterfly.

There is an exquisite significance in the changes of metaphor to describe the changes in the always winged love-thought (which is at the same time the love-act) from the sparrow to the robin and finally the butterfly spirit. First the gallant and laughing spirit of the sparrow as he speeds "under leaves so green." Then the bird of Calvary (like the weeping stars, or the sons of God shouting, broken-hearted for very joy) sweeps into the throbbing moment of Creation the whole gamut of earth's grief and heaven's rapture. The child wept with joy to hear the Piper's song, and the maiden hears, rather than feels, the beating of a joy too deep for thought as it seems to break in tears upon the crest of ecstatic realisation and accomplishment.

If the poem paints the experience of the maid, the illustration paints the male, and so the "wings" are transferred to the woman and what belongs to her. For, as the lover's love seemed winged thought to her— a vision and a voice from heaven—to the man it is the maiden herself who is an angelic vision or ideal, and this more especially as it concerns her motherhood, which, in the moment of the love-act, is still only realised in thought.

We must examine more closely these delicate spirits in love's crest, which are seven in number and move in clockwise motion[3] (always significant for Blake of the passage through life-experience to beatitude). The first spirit descends joyously (but without wings), the second finds its home "near my bosom" in the lap of the future mother, and is also unwinged. These are the sparrow and the robin

[3] *Cf.* the seven angels on the title-page of the "Job."

[4] Remembering the pulsing tears of the Robin, we can follow Blake's line of thought more closely when he wrote in the "Auguries of Innocence":

> Every Tear from Every Eye
> Becomes a Babe in Eternity
> This is caught by Females bright
> And returnd to its own delight.

from the male point of view, the gallant and joyous approach and the broken rapture of conquering surrender.[4] But after conception and birth (in vision as yet, and therefore winged) begins once more the round of Innocence and Experience from which life springs again. This is told in three scenes. Immediately beyond the Mother is a little cherub seated firmly on the parental stem and poring over a book.[5] The next figure stands erect and is summoned upwards by one still higher, and the last two meet in a paradise of love which is to renew the happy circle of life. We can almost hear Blake saying: "Ah! my child, I see you there reading my 'happy songs,' but the day will come when the songs are your own and your heaven is not a picture-book, but the paradise of another's bosom."

In the poem and in the picture there is so pervading an element of the ideal and of the visionary that one might be tempted to think the whole drama was a purely spiritual one with no basis upon earth, were it not, firstly, for the definite symbolism of the green leaves, which indicate the bodily life; and, secondly, for the unmistakable significance of the swift "arrow" and the "narrow" cradle, poetic symbols of the male and female organs. But though the drama is certainly in the flesh it is equally in the spirit, for "Man has no Body distinct from his Soul." [6] The symbolism and the very form of the verse suggest a bodily and a spiritual union, complete and secure, of the passive and the active element of love, the maid and the man. The illustrations to these companion poems "Infant Joy" and "The Blossom" each represent one of these aspects completed. The father's love-messenger brought benediction into the holy chamber of the mother's flower—the mother-vision wings blessing upon the father's spring of passion.

"Infant Joy" and "The Blossom" were placed facing one another in the first issue of the completed work ("S.I.E."), an issue in several ways significant.[7] Blake's success in weaving these poems and pictures (if it is success for an artist to perfect a work of art for himself alone) may have had a decisive effect upon his career, begetting that hard saying, uttered some years later, that "Allegory addressed to the Intellectual powers while it is altogether hidden from the Corporeal Understanding is My Definition of the Most Sublime Poetry" (Letter, July 6, 1803).

[5] It will be remembered that Job and his family in their days of Innocence are studying books. *Vide* Damon, p. 226, and Wicksteed's "Job," p. 90.
[6] "The Marriage," p. 4.
[7] *Vide supra*, p. 115, note, and *infra*, "A Little Girl Lost," p. 160.

Robert F. Gleckner: Spring

The connection between *Spring* and *The Ecchoing Green* is obviously very close despite the fact that Blake persistently kept the two apart in his issues of the songs. Apparently he used *Spring* many times as a contrasting poem, for in fifteen issues before 1815 it appears in connection with *On Another's Sorrow, The Blossom, The School Boy* (before its transference to *Experience*), *The Little Black Boy, Holy Thursday,* and *The Chimney Sweeper;* after 1815 it follows *Night.* In none of these poems does springtime play a major role except as a contrasting element. But *Spring* is more than merely an element in the contrast between happiness and sorrow, despite its apparent insouciance. Its more serious purpose is comparable to Blake's implied drama in the second stanza of *The Ecchoing Green.*

The anonymous command opening the poem ("Sound the Flute!") may be read simply as the breaking of the dark silence of the long night, the awakening of spring after winter's sleep, the revival of sport on the green after a night in the earthly mother's warm, protective bosom. In any case the rest of the stanza Blake devotes to a favorite subject, the birds of the air and the "bush," just as the next stanza belongs to the boy and girl, and the third to the lamb and "I." This type of Blakean progression also forms a prominent part of the structure of *Night* and the *Introduction,* and it is a good example of the way in which various symbols contribute to the formation of a major symbol, as well as of the process I have called shifting identity. In *Spring* the birds welcoming in the new year are the same birds that sing in *The Ecchoing Green,* that laugh in *Laughing Song,* that sport in the sky in *Nurse's Song,* that seek their nests in *Night,* that smile and cry in *The Blossom.* But they are also, specifically, a nightingale and a lark, a bird of the bush and a bird of the air, a bird of the night and a bird of the day. Blake thus establishes a dichotomy while at the same time maintaining the essential unity of the opposites in their identical response to the flute. Both birds sing, both delight, both welcome in the year. The joy of heralding spring is thus universalized so that the idea of renascence, as in *The*

Ecchoing Green, can be applied equally well to divinity, humanity, and the animal world.

In the second stanza the dichotomy is translated into human terms, the boy and girl, a technique used also in *The Ecchoing Green, Nurse's Song,* and *The Blossom.* Both boy and girl echo the welcome of stanza 1 with what Blake now calls infant noise, something undoubtedly like "the sweet chorus of Ha, Ha, He" in *Laughing Song.* There is nothing articulate as yet except insofar as joy is inherent in a wordless cry of ecstasy. Infancy in all its innocence and animality is another way to welcome in the year, to celebrate the awakening not merely of spring but of the human body (and soul), to commemorate the birth of the infant joy into the long day of sport on the green. The last stanza then goes beyond the simple, obvious comparison to unify the whole poem by resolving the two dominant images or "sets of characters," and synthesizing the diverse particulars which make up the universal welcome.

Though the last stanza begins on the same note as stanza 2, Blake introduces two new characters, the lamb and "I." If the comparison already in force between bird and child is expanded to include these lines, the poem resolves itself into something of an epic simile: as the birds delight and the boy and girl "crow" with infant noise, so we, the lamb and I, welcome in the year. Yet the "I" is not identified, except possibly as Blake himself, the lamb's appearance is unprepared for, and the mode of welcome in the last stanza differs greatly from those of the first two stanzas. This latter difference is due to the dichotomy already established between nightingale and lark, boy and girl: the first pair "delight," the second "crow" with "Merry voice." And capitalizing on the awakening of the body and soul in stanza 2 and the existence in the poem of male and female, the unmistakable tactile quality of the third stanza particularizes the random joy of the first two stanzas in the idea that "we" *love* to welcome in the year, love in the very limited sense applicable to ignorant, instinctive innocence. The tumult of the first two stanzas has now ceased, and in its place Blake evokes the sensuality of tongue on white neck, the softness of white wool, and the physical excitement of a kiss. In other words renascence is essentially a physical phenomenon in innocence. After having heard the herald and joined their infant sounds to the paean, the children become articulate in the awakening of physical desire. It is not necessary to read Freud into the lines but merely to recognize, as Blake did, that children's sport is physical as well as selfish. "Thoughtless" is Blake's word. Just as the song of a bird and the cry of a child is expended energy unrestrained, so the expression of bodily contact is divine energy in another form, the "sensual enjoyment" that must be "improv'd" before regeneration is possible. Blake's choice of the nightingale in the first stanza is therefore most apt: the male sings during the breeding season, the "energetic" season one might say. The entire last stanza concerns action, not contemplation, gratified desire not rationality.

The use of the first person, finally, shows Blake at his subtle best, in the reunification of what he has broken in two. "I" is at once the voice of both birds and both children, the latter now articulate; and the voice can be only one, the Piper's. In fact the entire structure of *Spring* is similar to that of the *Introduction:* the aimless piping in the latter parallels the birds' song in *Spring;* the piping of a song about a specific subject parallels the human voices of stanza 2; the addition of words to the Piper's music as the human voice replaces the pipe parallels the entire last stanza of *Spring;* and finally the union of inspiration, poet, Piper, and lamb also parallels the last stanza here. The parallels are inexact, of course, but the similarity goes even further. The command of stanza 1 in *Spring* is fundamentally the same as that delivered by the child on a cloud to the Piper; and *Spring* as a whole can easily be considered as the song about a lamb. This is precisely why Blake introduced the lamb into this poem at all. Where else could he have turned for a more appropriate symbol of rejuvenation and renascence than to the Lamb of God? Reawakening, then, is spiritual as well as physical. For Blake the two were identical, an improvement in sensual enjoyment being synonymous with regeneration.

Harold Bloom: Holy Thursday

On Ascension Day the charity children are led into St. Paul's to celebrate the charity of God, that loving pity of which human charity is intended as a direct reflection. The voice of this song is not a child's, but rather of a self-deceived onlooker, impressed by a palpable vision of Innocence, moved by these flowers of London town. The flowing metre is gently idyllic, and the singer gives us two

"Holy Thursday," by Harold Bloom. (Title supplied by the editor.) From Blake's Apocalypse: A Study in Poetic Argument (New York: Doubleday, 1963), pp. 44–45. Copyright © 1963, by Harold Bloom. Reprinted by permission of Doubleday & Company, Inc.

stanzas of Innocent sight, followed by the triumphant sound of Innocence raising its voice to Heaven.

The ambiguity of tone of Blake's songs is never more evident than here, and yet never more difficult to evidence. One can point of course to several disturbing details. The children's faces have been scrubbed clean, and are innocent, in a debased sense—because they ought to appear brutalized, which they are, and yet do not. The children are regimented; they walk two and two, and the beadles' wands are both badges of office and undoubtedly instruments of discipline in a savage British scholastic tradition. The children are dressed in the colors of life; the beadles are grey-headed and carry white as a death emblem. It is the fortieth day after Easter Sunday, forty days after Christ's ascension into Heaven, yet the children, his Lambs, still linger unwillingly in the wilderness of an exploiting society. Though they flow like Thames' waters, this is not a mark of their freedom but of the binding of the Thames, which is already the "chartered" river of the poem *London* in *Songs of Experience*. The prophet Joel, crying that man's wickedness was great, called for "multitude, multitudes in the valley of decision." The hum of multitudes is in St. Paul's, but these are multitudes of lambs, and their radiance is "all their own"; it has nothing to do with the Church. Their voice rises like a wind of judgment, and thunders harmoniously among the seats of Heaven. *Beneath* the children, spiritually as well as actually, are the seats of Heaven upon which sit the beadles. If these guardians of the poor are wise, it is not with the wisdom of Innocence, and their wisdom is epitomized in the last line, at once one of the bitterest in Blake by its context, and one of the most seemingly Innocent in its content.

Mark Schorer: Experience

The forms of bondage, especially the bondage of "sexual strife," are the chief ingredients of the *Songs of Experience*. They develop out of the second, the humanitarian, element of the *Poetical Sketches,* but they are expressed now with that intensity which is the particular mark of Blake's genius, and without contradiction.

"Experience," by Mark Schorer. (Title supplied by the editor.) From William Blake: The Politics of Vision *(New York: Henry Holt, 1946), pp. 237–38. Copyright 1946 by Holt, Rinehart and Winston, Inc.*

The children of *Songs of Innocence* have become captives who cry for liberty, and, denied it, suffer a deterioration of natural virtue. The onslaughts of authority and the moral consequence begin at once, in infancy:

> Struggling in my father's hands,
> Striving against my swadling bands,
> Bound and weary I thought best
> To sulk upon my mother's breast.

The onslaughts of authority continue. "The Schoolboy" reminds us not only of Blake's resistance to education but of the Godwinian assault on it as the root of prejudice. Religion listens to the little lost boy's intuition that man is godly and that God is human, and burns him as a heretic, which is to say that in experience, dogma destroys intuition. The same child, perhaps, pleads in "The Little Vagabond" that the free pleasures of the alehouse are more desirable than the repressions of the Church, which decrees good and evil in its law. The protest in all these poems is against authority because it ignores individuality by restraining natural impulse. The impulse that is most emphatically in Blake's mind becomes evident in the yearnings for liberty of the young man and woman in "Ah! Sun-flower":

> . . . the Youth pined away with desire,
> And the pale Virgin shrouded in snow.

The bulk of the poems in *Songs of Experience* are directed against the conventional restraints imposed upon sexuality. That mistaken attitudes toward sexual love are made the root of all the errors in experience is not surprising when one remembers Blake's final comment on Lavater. The infant who learns to "sulk" immediately is a creature not out of Lavater's psychology but out of Freud's.

Hazard Adams: The Two Nurse's Songs

The issue is what kind of relation can exist between the self and its emanations. It is obvious that one argument attempts to negate the other. The first tends toward what Blake would call the "religious"

"*The Two Nurse's Songs,*" *by Hazard Adams. (Title supplied by the editor.) From* William Blake: A Reading of the Shorter Poems *(Seattle: University of Washington Press, 1963), pp. 252–55. Reprinted by permission of the publisher.*

view. It leads to a rejection of sensual pleasure, perhaps to a desire for martyrdom. The second is its cynical negation. It sees love as self-gratification, the ultimate imposition of restraint upon the other through the desire for possession. The clod of clay argues that only in giving is there love. The pebble proposes that giving becomes keeping or taking. It is not merely the similarity of a phrase in the pebble's speech to lines in "The Mental Traveller" which suggests that there is something cyclical in all of this. We are led to seek for a joining of these views in the form of contraries rather than negations.

The poems to be discussed in this chapter examine various clod- and pebble-like attitudes and variations upon these attitudes, ranging from forms of innocence to forms of experience. We begin to learn the flaws in each state when we are able to observe it alone and in detail. Our subject is more specifically those pairs of poems from *Innocence* and *Experience* with similar titles. The two nurses' songs provide an excellent beginning:

> When the voices of children are heard on the green
> And laughing is heard on the hill,
> My heart is at rest within my breast
> And everything else is still
>
> Then come home my children the sun is gone down
> And the dews of night arise
> Come come leave off play, and let us away
> Till the morning appears in the skies
>
> No no let us play, for it is yet day
> And we cannot go to sleep
> Besides in the sky, the little birds fly
> And the hills are all coverd with sheep
>
> Well well go & play till the light fades away
> And then go home to bed
> The little one leaped & shouted & laugh'd
> And all the hills ecchoed

(*Innocence*)

> When the voices of children, are heard on the green
> And whisprings are in the dale:
> The days of my youth rise fresh in my mind,
> My face turns green and pale.

Then come home my children, the sun is gone down
And the dews of night arise
Your spring & your day, are wasted in play
And your winter and night in disguise.

(*Experience*)

The second nurse's journey into experience has stolen from her all
intimations of the reality of innocence. She would like to think the
state of innocence a real condition, but her passage to experience was
apparently such a disillusionment that she has made a negation of
innocence. This same cynicism is apparent in the pebble's statement.
According to the pebble, the real form of love—the experience form—
is self-love. In her disillusionment, the nurse has come to believe the
pebble correct. Ironically, however, it is her own cynicism which
proves the pebble's point; for her mental state is completely egocen-
tric. She is locked in her own being, her own troubles; and she attempts
to draw the children into them. Her delight might well be described
as "another's loss of ease." She is the kind of person who is always lamenting the passage of time, but in her present condition she would
find no joy even in a rediscovered past.

The poem's language is simple and conventional. The nurse sees
the passage of a single day as representative of the passage from youth
to age, from a joy based upon cruel "innocent" self-deception to a
more cruel reality. The coming of night and the falling of dew, reminiscent of the "vapour" in "The Little Boy Lost," are to her a perverse sort of baptism into these realities. Reading from this point of
view, we must conclude that Blake's nurse is meant to be bitter and
histrionic, and thus sentimental. Perhaps this is the reason for the
strange exaggeration of "my face turns green and pale," a line severely
criticized by G. K. Chesterton as inaccurate. The inaccuracy is that
of the speaker, not Blake. The speaker bitterly exaggerates everything
else in the poem in a self-pitying mannr. Her histrionics are revealed
not simply in the line Chesterton disliked, but in her total gesture.
I think it is fair to associate the mental state of the *Experience* nurse
with Urizen in the process of creating his own mental hell:

Dark, revolving in silent activity:
Unseen in tormenting passions:
An activity unknown and horrible,
A self-contemplating shadow.

(*K223*)

The nurse of *Innocence* reacts quite differently to what we can suppose is the same situation. Some of the subtleties of both poems are revealed by the contrast between them. Neither poem would be quite the same without the other. Let us look again at the first three lines of both. The whisperings heard by the jaded nurse of *Experience* show that she can invest anything with the slightly sinister. Such a suggestion is created partially by the contrasting line in *Innocence,* not completely in the confines of its own form. And, too the reminiscence of youth in the third line of the second poem is made to seem more clearly a sign of weakness by the existence of the first nurse's words. For her, time suspends itself in the joyful moment. For this reason she seems not to resent time's passage, and she calls to the children with no bitterness. She knows that the descent is inevitable, but she does not see it as having been a cruel joke:

> Come come leave off play, and let us away
> Till the morning appears in the skies

The nurse of *Innocence* has not been overcome by experience, even though she has traveled in its areas. Her reaction to childish pleasure is calm, rather than jovial, and this probably accounts for the sadness noted by Wicksteed in his commentary on the poem. Yet the sadness is ours perhaps more than the nurse's. As the poem concludes, the nurse no longer speaks and the poet describes the hills echoing again to the children's cries. That final image restores the sense of animation in nature. For though the hills literally only reflect the sounds, nevertheless we tend to read the line metaphorically as we do when someone says, for instance, "He echoed my thoughts," and means that they found themselves in agreement.

> The little ones leaped & shouted & laugh'd
> And all the hills ecchoed

These two nurses must be thought of in relation to the lost, seeking mothers and lullaby singers of other songs. We see also behind the nurse of experience Little Mary Bell of the Pickering poems, who very definitely joyed for a time in another's loss of ease but was ultimately the loser. This sense of loss and cynical negation of innocence as a delusion as well as its related dangers is the subject of many verses from the Rossetti MS. There is the lament of the old maid:

> An old maid early eer I knew
> Ought but the love than on me grew

> And now Im covered oer & oer
> And wish that I had been a Whore

(*K*184)

And there is Blake's answer:

> He who bends to himself a joy
> Doth the winged life destroy
> But he who kisses the joy as it flies
> Lives in Eternity's sun rise

(*K*179)

This is not the "gather ye rosebuds" theme it appears to be. Such an interpretation would overlook the fact that lines 1 and 2 refer unmistakably to the ideas implicit in the pebble's analysis of love—the gratification of the self-hood's desire to dominate, which turns things down into the circle from which there is no escape.

Martin K. Nurmi: Blake's Revisions of *The Tyger*

It seems to me that the change of mood which we have observed Blake to pass through in his first two stages can be most easily accounted for as reflecting his responses to events in France in the late summer and early autumn of 1792. Several lines of evidence converge to suggest this: the date of the drafts, the historical echoes in the pivotal fifth stanza, and above all the fact that the course of the revolution in this period was such that it could—and did—arouse this kind of response among humanitarian republicans.

Such cruel excesses of revolutionary energy as the Rising of the 10th of August and the September Massacres furnish a plausible occasion for Blake's troubled mood in the first stage. There was always something of the "gentle visionary" about Blake, and he must have deplored these early terrors, despite his ardent Jacobinism. Though his apocalypses may sometimes stream with blood (e.g., the end of *Milton*), he preferred to think of revolutions as bloodless, hoping in *The French Revolution* that the struggle would end by the king's soldier simply embracing the "meek peasant." Even in *America,* where he must treat a military victory won by American armies, he would

Reprinted by permission of the Modern Language Association of America from "Blake's Revisions of The Tyger," *by Martin K. Nurmi. From* Publications of the Modern Language Association, *LXXI (1956), 681–83.*

rather not show the Americans as actually fighting; they merely "rush together," owing their victory to the fact of their solidarity and to the spiritual manifestation of revolution in the flaming Orc.

Then in late September came news that violence was apparently over, news which could have prompted the shift in mood seen in Blake's second stage. Viewed prophetically, such events as the defeat of the Austrians at Valmy on the 20th (to which Erdman, p. 178, has called attention in connection with the fifth stanza), the formation of the National Convention on the 21st, and the announcement of the French Republic on the 22nd must have made the attainment of Innocence seem close enough to cast the bloody actions of August and mid-September pretty well into the background. This view, according to Wordsworth and Coleridge, was even typical. The "lamentable crimes" of the September Massacres, writes Wordsworth, remembering the period after the announcement of the Republic,

> were past,
> Earth free from them for ever, as was thought,—
> Ephemeral monsters, to be seen but once!
> Things that could only show themselves and die.[1]

"The dissonance ceased," recalls Coleridge, "and all seemed calm and bright . . ." [2]

Blake is not, to be sure, writing merely a revolutionary lyric. His tiger is not another Orc, another portrayal of the spirit of revolt, but something much more inclusive, a symbol showing the creative power of energy, even of wrathful energy, wherever it appears. But because the revolution was for Blake a crucial contemporary manifestation of energy, events in the progress of the revolution would affect even his larger conception.[3]

[1] *Prelude* (1850), ed. Ernest de Selincourt (London, 1926), x.41–47.
[2] "France: An Ode," *Poems*, ed. Ernest Hartley Coleridge (London, 1912), p. 245.
[3] The Orc component of the tiger may be seen in the general similarities between the tiger and Orc in *America*, who, like the tiger, burns in the night as if he had been forged, glowing "as the wedge / Of iron heated in the furnace" (p. 202), and whose origin is a little ambiguously either in the Satanic deeps or the divine Atlantic mountains (p. 202). Very bloody revolutionary tigers indeed are associated with Orc in *Europe*, where Enitharmon's premature belief that Eden had come—a situation parallel to Blake's 2nd stage of composition—is shattered by the resumption of strife (p. 219). These tigers, however, are far removed from the tiger of the poem, representing a limit of this use of the symbol by Blake. Blake's later disillusionment with Orc in 1801 (as Napoleon—Erdman, p. 292) is parallel to his use of the "forms of tygers & of Lions" to show men "dishumaniz'd" by war in night VI of *The Four Zoas* (p. 303). [The edition of Blake cited is *Blake's Poetry and Prose*, ed. Geoffrey Keynes (London, 1948).—Ed.]

For Blake to have been thus affected by contemporary events, his Notebook would have had to lie idle for a period of ten days or even several weeks, since the MS. drafts are on successive pages. This is easily possible. He did not write in his Notebook exclusively or constantly, but used it at this time for lyrics, which, according to H. M. Margoliouth, were written in response to events of one kind or another.[4] Moreover, if his uncertainty concerning such an important concept as that of energy was unresolved during his first stage, it is unlikely that he could work very productively until it was resolved, in the second stage. That an interruption did occur is suggested, indeed, by the appearance of the pages of the MS.—and even the appearance of a MS. page could conceivably have had some significance for the inventor of "illuminated printing." Whereas the first draft ends a page crowded with lyrics, the other drafts occupy a page that is otherwise blank, except for a light sketch. The empty space at the top of the second page, coming after the profusion of poems on the first, thus seems a visual parallel to the mournful and unproductive "blank in Nature" declared by Los in *Milton* (p. 383).

Blake's last revision is another matter. The final poem cannot be accounted for as a response to specific events. Though the Terror of late 1792 and early 1793 could have shown him that his relatively mild tiger of the second stage was premature, his restoration of dreadfulness to the poem in its final version does not show the influence of events—and certainly not of events like the Terror—as do his exaggerations of the two earlier stages. On the contrary, Blake's being able to handle dreadfulness and assimilate it in the unified symmetry of the final poem shows him to gain precisely that control of his material which his concern with revolution seems to have prevented him from gaining in his earlier stages. He is now able to transcend the limitations of specific events and give his symbol the comprehensive scope of an "eternal principle." This is the result of hard thought, not of events. Blake can now give the tiger's dreadfulness symbolic distance because he can see it in a perspective in which it no longer has the immediacy of an issue. And he can portray its symmetry as containing a really fearful component because he can see clearly and fully, at this point, the place of the tiger in the divine plan.

---

[4] *William Blake* (London, 1951), p. 54. Margoliouth remarks that the occasion of *The Tyger* is unknown, but believes that this poem is occasional (p. 58).

E. D. Hirsch, Jr.: "The Human Abstract"

This poem is as central to the *Songs of Experience* as "The Divine Image" (the poem it satirizes) is to the *Songs of Innocence*. It begins as a point-for-point refutation of the touchstones of Innocence— Mercy, Pity, Peace, and Love—but moves quickly beyond this limited satire to present a bitter mythical account of the way the delusive values of Innocence have caused the Fall of man. The opening stanza, one of Blake's best attempts to satirize an earlier poem, should be read as if one of the Swedenborgian "Angels" were speaking. (One draft version, No. 8 of the Rossetti Manuscript, explicitly gives the lines to an "Angel.") In defending the values of Innocence, the Angel damns both them and himself:

> Pity would be no more [pronounced
>   as an unthinkable calamity]
> If we did not make somebody Poor.
> And Mercy no more could be [an even
>   greater calamity]
> If all were as happy as we.

In accepting that this is an ineluctably suffering world, Innocence had celebrated the sacramental quality of Mercy and Pity. But the love from which these divine attributes arise demands more than passive sympathy with another's sorrow; it demands active alleviation of sorrow as well, and this was a point that Innocence had failed to urge with sufficient force. It thus left itself open to the accusation that it valued pious complacency and self-gratulation above active social betterment. The accusation is not altogether fair, and since Innocence was to have the last word in Blake's final version of the *Songs*, it should be pointed out that the accusation is itself rather vulnerable. When all men are released from the Urizenic bonds, will there be no more misery? If you abolish poverty, do you really abolish the need of pity? Even though the cut worm forgives the plow, is there to be no compassion for pain? for failure? old age? death? The underside of Blake's attack is the sanguine and touchingly naïve revolutionary faith that all would be "as happy as we" if only the whole unnatural edifice built with Mercy and Pity and the rest were to crumble.

In the second stanza Blake quickly drops the angelic mask and converts the two remaining divine attributes of Innocence to something overtly sinister:

> And mutual fear brings peace
> Till the selfish loves increase.

The dropping of the mask is preparation for Blake's naturalistic myth of the Fall, which like the traditional myth involves a tree. Blake was fond of allegorical trees. The symbols of roots, branches, fruits, and roosting birds are all to be found in *Poetical Sketches* ("Love and Harmony Combine") and the association of the tree with the Fall is central, of course, to "A Poison Tree." Blake preserved his favorite images, but the fallacy of attaching the same kind of meaning to each recurrent use of them should be apparent to anyone who compares the symbolic tree of this poem with that of "Love and Harmony Combine." Blake's tree also illustrates the pointlessness of insisting that his poetry is "mythic," which is to say trans-intellectual, archetypal, and, in short, good, rather than "allegorical," which is to say intellectual, self-conscious, and, in short, bad. Blake's tree, like most images in his poetry, is mythical and allegorical at the same time. Like any poet risen above the level of primitive culture, Blake attaches definite conceptions to his myths and thereby converts them to allegories.

In this poem every image has precise conceptual correspondences. The seed of the fatal tree is "Cruelty"—the cruelty implied in the Angel's desire to keep people poor and unhappy. Within the trap he has baited, Cruelty waters with crocodile tears the seed he has formed. Blake's horticultural knowledge was precise. First the root forms from the seed—the root of "Humility"—but it is the false humility of the "humble sheep" who displays a "threat'ning horn" ("The Lilly"). Then the epicotyl develops into leaves and branches—into the dismal shade of Mystery. Next

> the Catterpiller and Fly
> Feed on the Mystery.

The priestly caterpillar who benefits from human repression has been encountered before:

> As the catterpiller chooses the fairest leaves to lay her
> eggs on, so the priest lays his curse on the fairest joys.
>
> ("Proverbs of Hell")

Then, the stage of flowering being wisely skipped over, the tree

> bears the fruit of deceit
> Ruddy and sweet to eat.

Of course, the fruit is sweet, just as Eve's apple was, but its sweetness is entirely in its secret, hypocritical, and mouth-watering voluptuousness. Finally, the denizen of this tree is the Raven—the symbol of death, for the tree is the epitome of all that is life-denying and life-destroying.

Blake calls this image a "Human Abstract" because it is the history of an illusion. The tree of religion is an entirely human invention, like Locke's philosophy. It is a "cloven fiction" built up by dividing the mental from the actual, the human from the natural. The tree is thus "abstract" in the same way that to Wordsworth and Coleridge the false, secondary powers of the mind are abstract. Blake is giving his own version of the distinction between "fancy" or "understanding" on the one side and "imagination" on the other, between operations of the mind in disconnection and isolation, and operations which are in alliance with the larger reality. Imagination or vision, being a fusion of the mind with this larger reality, is authentic and true, while fancy or abstraction is unauthentic and false. To put the matter as simply as possible, Blake calls the tree of religion an "abstract" because it is the consequence of the mind's turning, like Urizen, upon itself. The concrete reality Blake opposes to this abstract is Nature. His statement is as explicit as possible:

> The Gods of the earth and sea
> Sought thro' Nature to find this Tree.
> But their search was all in vain.
> There grows one in the human brain.

The appeal to Nature had been implicit from the beginning of the poem. That pity should be no more is a natural condition, because pity is founded on an artificiality. We "make" somebody poor. Our trust in instinct and the natural order is perverted by "mutual fears." And all the components of the tree—Humility, Mystery, Deceit—are unnatural in precisely the same way. They create a separate human world that has nothing to do with the fundamental reality—the universal, exuberant, self-delighting impulse of life. That reality is what

Blake has in mind when he says, "every thing that lives is holy." That reality is also what he means in this poem when he uses the word "Nature."

This satire of "The Divine Image" thus turns out to be a poem that affirms a religious faith as powerful as the one expressed in the poem it satirizes. And the faith it expresses was derived from the very religion against which it directs its irony. The subject of "The Divine Image" had been the indwelling presence of the divine:

> Where Mercy, Love & Pity dwell
> There God is dwelling too.

Now, abandon the idea of a mediating Christ, and leave out of account the transcendent reality that sanctions this immanental faith, and the result is the conviction that

> All deities reside in the human breast.

That statement implies, among other things, that the "human brain" can choose to make the world the glorious place it implicitly is, or can create a falsely isolated and therefore fallen world. It can make a god that is repressive of holy instincts or it can make a god out of those holy instincts themselves. The deity that resides in the human breast *can* be the true deity—that is, the divine life in man and nature. "The Human Abstract" is not just a satire of "The Divine Image" but also a naturalization of it. The same immanental faith runs through both, and this is important to notice because it discloses one of the main currents in the astonishing spiritual development to which we owe the existence of the *Songs*.

The Design. Below the text, Urizen squats on the ground as if rooted there. Out of his head grow ropelike branches that appear to hold him prisoner as his hands struggle against them. As in the design to "London" Urizen is both the cause and the victim of his bondage.

Chronology of Important Dates

Blake		The Age	
1757	Blake born.		
1772– 1779	Apprenticeship as engraver to James Basire.	1775– 1781	American Revolution.
		1779	Hume, *Dialogues Concerning Natural Religion.*
1782	Marries Catherine Boucher.	1781– 1788	Rousseau, *Confessions.*
1783	*Poetical Sketches,* his first book, is printed.		
1784 or 1785	Writes *An Island in the Moon.*		
1788	First etched works: *There Is No Natural Religion, All Religions Are One.*		
1789	Begins to etch *Songs of Innocence* and *The Book of Thel.*	1789	Fall of Bastille; French Revolution.
1790– 1792	Notebook drafts of *Songs of Experience.*	1792	September massacres. Battle of Valmy; revolutionary victories. Republic proclaimed.
1793	Issues prospectus advertising illuminated works, including both sets of *Songs,*	1793	England and France at war; Reign of Terror. Godwin, *Political Justice.*

	Thel, America, The Marriage of Heaven and Hell, and *Visions of the Daughters of Albion.*		
		1794	State Trials of British radical leaders.
1793–1800	Residence in Lambeth.	1798	Wordsworth and Coleridge, *Lyrical Ballads.*
c. 1797–1805	Works on *The Four Zoas.*	1799	Napoleon's coup of 18th Brumaire.
1800–1803	Residence at Felpham, Sussex.	Oct. 1801–May 1803	Peace of Amiens.
1803	Indicted for sedition.	1802	Napoleon made Consul for life.
1804	Tried at Chichester and acquitted.	1804	Napoleon crowned Emperor.
		1805	Death of Nelson.
		1806	Death of Pitt.
		1807	Abolition of slave trade.
1809	Exhibits his paintings at his brother's.		
1809 or 1810	Publishes *Milton.*		
		1814–1815	Congress of Vienna.
		1815	Waterloo.
1818–1820	Publishes *Jerusalem.*		
		1819	"Peterloo" massacre.
1825	*Illustrations of the Book of Job.*		
1827	Dies at 2 Fountain Court, Strand.		

Notes on the Editor and Contributors

MORTON D. PALEY (University of California, Berkeley) has written a study of the development of Blake's thought, *Energy and the Imagination,* published by the Clarendon Press. He is editor of the *Blake Newsletter.*

HAZARD ADAMS, in addition to having written the critical study of Blake's lyrics from which our excerpt is taken, is the author of *Blake and Yeats: the Contrary Vision* and of *The Contexts of Poetry.* He is chairman of the English Department at the University of California, Irvine.

HAROLD BLOOM (Yale University) has published three books on poets of the Romantic period: *Shelley's Mythmaking, The Visionary Company,* and *Blake's Apocalypse.* He is also co-editor of the critical anthology *From Sensibility to Romanticism.*

S. FOSTER DAMON is the pioneer of Blake studies in America. His monumental *William Blake: His Philosophy and Symbols* first appeared in 1924; his *Blake Dictionary* was published in 1965. He has also written two books on series of designs by Blake: *Blake's Job* and *Blake's Grave.* He is Professor of English at Brown University.

DAVID V. ERDMAN (State University of New York, Stony Brook) edited the most up-to-date and useful text of Blake's writings, *The Poetry and Prose of William Blake.* He is now preparing a new edition of his influential study *Blake: Prophet Against Empire.* He is editor of the *Bulletin* of the New York Public Library.

NORTHROP FRYE is the author of *Anatomy of Criticism,* perhaps the most important work of critical theory of our time. In addition to his brilliant *Fearful Symmetry,* he has written books on Shakespeare, Milton, and, most recently, English romanticism. He is Principal of Massey College, University of Toronto.

ROBERT F. GLECKNER is Chairman of the English Department at the University of California, Riverside. Our selection is taken from his book on Blake's *Songs, The Piper and the Bard.* He recently published *Byron and the Ruins of Paradise.*

E. D. HIRSCH's most recent book is *Validity in Interpretation*. He also wrote *Wordsworth and Schelling: a Typological Study of Romanticism*. He teaches at Yale University.

MARTIN K. NURMI (Kent State University) is co-author (with Gerald E. Bentley, Jr.) of the indispensable *Blake Bibliography*. He has also written a monograph on *The Marriage of Heaven and Hell* as well as numerous articles and reviews.

ALICIA OSTRIKER has written on Tennyson and on Wyatt and Surrey, in addition to her work on Blake's prosody. She teaches at Rutgers University.

MARTIN PRICE is the author of *To the Palace of Wisdom* and *Swift's Rhetorical Art*. He is Professor of English at Yale University.

MARK SCHORER, author of *Sinclair Lewis: An American Life*, is one of America's best-known literary critics. His latest book is *The World We Imagine*. He teaches at the University of California, Berkeley.

JOSEPH H. WICKSTEED pioneered in the study of the symbolism of Blake's illustrations, with his *Blake's Vision of the Book of Job*, first published in 1910. He also wrote a book-length study of Blake's *Jerusalem*, brought out by the Blake Trust in 1953.

Selected Bibliography

Blake, William, *Songs of Innocence and of Experience* (New York: Orion Press, 1967). A color facsimile of Blake's original, with editorial comments by Sir Geoffrey Keynes. This book gives us the *Songs* as Blake intended them to be read—with the accompanying illustrations.

Damon, S. Foster, *A Blake Dictionary* (Providence, R.I.: Brown University Press, 1965). A rich compendium of articles, short and long, about Blake's works, ideas, and symbols, arranged in dictionary form.

England, Martha Winburn, "Blake and the Hymns of Charles Wesley," *Bulletin* of the New York Public Library, LXX (1966), 7–33. A valuable, full discussion of the relation of the *Songs* to Wesley's *Hymns for Children*.

Frye, Northrop (Ed.), *Blake: A Collection of Critical Essays* (Englewood Cliffs, N.J.: Prentice-Hall, 1966). Includes "Point of View and Context in Blake's Songs," by Robert F. Gleckner; "Fact and Symbol in 'The Chimney Sweeper' of Blake's *Songs of Innocence*," by Martin K. Nurmi; "Interpreting Blake's 'The Fly,'" by John E. Grant; "The Complexities of Blake's 'Sunflower': An Archetypal Speculation," by William J. Keith; "Little Girls Lost: Problems of a Romantic Archetype," by Irene H. Chayes.

Gilchrist, Alexander, *The Life of William Blake,* rev. ed., ed. Ruthven Todd (London: J. M. Dent, 1945). A scholarly edition of the first and still the most interesting biography of Blake.

Grant, John E., "The Art and Argument of 'The Tyger,'" *Texas Studies in Language and Literature,* II (1960), 38–60.

Landry, Hilton, "The Symbolism of Blake's Sunflower," *Bulletin* of the New York Public Library, LXVI (1962), 613–19.

Miner, Paul, "'The Tyger': Genesis and Evolution in the Poetry of William Blake," *Criticism* IV (1962), 59–73.

Rosenfeld, Alvin (Ed.), *William Blake: Essays and Studies for S. Foster Damon* (Providence, R.I.: Brown University Press, 1969). Includes "Two Flowers in the Garden of Experience" by John E. Grant and "Blake's 'The Fly'" by Jean H. Hagstrum.

TWENTIETH CENTURY
INTERPRETATIONS

MAYNARD MACK, *Series Editor*
Yale University

NOW AVAILABLE
Collections of Critical Essays
ON

(continued on next page)

(*continued from previous page*)

HENRY IV, PART TWO
HENRY V
THE ICEMAN COMETH
JULIUS CAESAR
KEATS'S ODES
LORD JIM
MUCH ADO ABOUT NOTHING
OEDIPUS REX
THE OLD MAN AND THE SEA
PAMELA
THE PLAYBOY OF THE WESTERN WORLD
THE PORTRAIT OF A LADY
A PORTRAIT OF THE ARTIST AS A YOUNG MAN
PRIDE AND PREJUDICE
THE RAPE OF THE LOCK
THE RIME OF THE ANCIENT MARINER
ROBINSON CRUSOE
SAMSON AGONISTES
THE SCARLET LETTER
SIR GAWAIN AND THE GREEN KNIGHT
SONGS OF INNOCENCE AND OF EXPERIENCE
THE SOUND AND THE FURY
THE TEMPEST
TESS OF THE D'URBERVILLES
TOM JONES
TWELFTH NIGHT
UTOPIA
VANITY FAIR
WALDEN
THE WASTE LAND
WUTHERING HEIGHTS